The Trawler

2020

Gloucestershire Poetry Society
Anthology of Selected Poems

Black Eyes Publishing UK

The Trawler 2020
Gloucestershire Poetry Society Anthology of Selected Poems
© Peter Lay 2020

Published by Black Eyes Publishing UK, 2020
Brockworth, Gloucestershire, England
www.blackeyespublishinguk.co.uk

ISBN: 9781913195120

A CIP catalogue record for this title is available from the British Library.

Editor: Josephine Lay
                     www.thegloucestershirepoetrysociety.com

Cover design: Jason Conway, cre8urbrand.
                     www.cre8urbrand.co.uk

Introduction

This collection of poetry is different to the norm: these poems have been taken (trawled) from the Gloucestershire Poetry Society (GPS) group Facebook pages. Some of them are rough diamonds, still in need of cutting, polishing or setting, but never the less they're diamonds and of sufficient value to be included within these pages. Here are 100 poems (posted between January 2019 and May 2020) by 47 poets. Many of these poems are first drafts, some are by erudite poets, and some by people who have just begun writing, but each poem has an element - style, voice, content or passion - that called to us as we read it.

The GPS was set up in 2016 by Ziggy Slug, AKA, the poet Z. D. Dicks; our present Gloucestershire Poet Laureate. Ziggy envisaged a forum where membership would be free and where members could post their poems without judgement and/or critique, unless specifically asked for, but where some feedback could be gained. This opportunity to air new work without affecting the poem's chances of publication (as it is posted in a closed group) has worked very successfully.

In January 2020 Ziggy passed the running of the GPS over to myself, Josephine Lay, and Jason Conway. We had some new ideas as to how the GPS could move forward, one of which was the possible publication of some of our group's poetry. The Covid-19 pandemic put most of our plans on hold, but the trawling of poems from the group Facebook page was unaffected so, in conjunction with Peter Lay of Black Eyes Publishing UK, we have collated this collection of poems.

I hope you'll enjoy these varied poems posted out of enthusiasm for the written word, some from as far away as New Zealand, Australia and the Caribbean. We have not edited them (other than to spell check and alter basic punctuation) and I hope they'll give a flavour of our many Gloucestershire Poetry Society members throughout the UK and the rest of the world.

Josephine Lay   September 2020

The Trawler

2020

Jonathan Robert Muirhead

1978 ~ 2020

Contents

Marilyn Timms

A Day Like Any Other
Written after walking in a Cheltenham park last summer (2019)

Another burnt-toast day begins –
satchels, car keys, lost and found
inner-city buses chased and lost.
Teenagers share a needle, share a can
can't imagine growing old.
Beside the fountain in the park
crusaders plant a garden for the dispossessed
erect a placard 'HELP YOURSELVES!'
never question how marjoram might help
with hoarding lives in plastic bags.
Unseen beneath the willow trees
a cardboard chrysalis splits and spills
a man upon the grass to wait, a patient butterfly,
until the meagre sun can warm his blood.
A car backfires, a sniper sound
that drives him back to Desert Storm,
awakens pain in his missing leg,
reminds him how he loved to dance.
Later, he hijacks a doorway near the bank,
dines on second-hand kebabs.
Spare some change, guv? Anything?
Any spare change? The entire town
bears witness to a modern miracle —
the unknown soldier is become invisible.

Stephen Moore

A Drought of Words

For a while, our washing machine would move around when spinning a full load. Hearing it, reminded me of how sometimes, my mind needs to settle, be stilled and thoughts washed and aired to dry.

A drought of words on paper,
My head a locked, off balance, washing machine,
Stuffed with thoughts,

Rolling,
Churning,
Crashing across a floor.

Till at last, the cycle returns to drain,
Dry,
Air.

Matty Blades

A Gentle Walk

In the countryside I glide
My cares all drift away

The birds tweet a beautiful melody
That are drowned out by the city noise
A gentle walk
All peaceful and calm
My soul it does seem to be free
All my worries seem to bleed away
Whilst walking amongst the trees
Hear the whispers on the breeze
Through the leaves it blows
The creaking of the branches speak
As they slowly grow
Peace abounds
My soul set free
Awakening myself to me.

Matty Blades

A Little Hope

Just as I think it's going ok
So again, wakes up the pain
A torrent of memories plague me
As I relive it again and again
Clawing away at my fractured mind
This insidious mental disease
Tearing away any semblance of self
And setting my demons free
Wound up so tight
It feels like I could explode
But somewhere deep inside of me
There must be a little hope
A spark of creativity
A way to release the pain
To pour my heart upon the page
To stop myself going insane.

Clive Oseman

Alone

This is it, the grim reality.
The road to insanity is paved
with days like this
when the kiss of loneliness
is the only one you get
and your thoughts stay in your head,
because there's no one to hear them if they are said.

This is when it really hits.
You could pick up the phone
and tell a distant friend
how you are in bits
how you need someone to talk to
and for sure they would listen,
their lives burdened with this shit
they have no power to change,
and I could kid myself this wasn't strange.

Instead, I write deep into the night,
tell myself that I'm alright,
how one day I will find new life,
then I turn off the light,
close my eyes,
concede the fight.

Clive Oseman

Am I awake

or is all this just a nightmare
from which there's no escape?
It's hard to tell.
I'm used to awful dreams
but this one just seems different,
like I'm in solitary confinement
and the window to the world
shows a silent movie
where death and fear stalk humanity
so, they drive us to insanity
as a cure.
I'm not sure.
There's no one to ask.
It's 3 am but feels no different
to all the hours past.
I look at social media, aghast.
It seems it's all too real
and the emptiness I feel
is matched by everyone.
Normality has gone
and Facebook's full of experts
knowing who or what to blame for certain.
But none of it makes sense.
I'll make a cup of tea,
have a conversation with myself
the only person there for me
right now.
Then I'll do some reading,
find something that's worth believing,
and hope.

Vicky Hampton

An Impotent Year

January is a clag clinging to the sticks.
It makes the old stove's glass slow
to clear of soot. But still I sit, feed the heat
from the ruins of the year around my feet

and in the gradual roar, its diary's sheets
glow whiter than they ever were,
becoming, in the end, a speechless sun
behind a muted mound of clouds. And

I'm hard put to see how something inane
as a page burns with such intelligence,
how violence fashions the delicacy of ash,
and how that level of energy is contained

the way anger on paper is (done with flair).
For I'd not written even one thing there.

Ben Poppy

As I've Grown Happier

The world has grown sadder
Everyone else has locked themselves away
Before I left an empty home for empty Holborn
Before a walk through an empty Trafalgar Square
I have found myself alone
And there's no one left in Camden Town
You can't hear the musicians play
Some are hiding with their creation
Some are suffering from isolation
And I had felt the same in a small cafe
With each drop of whisky onto ice
Before I found you
Those eyes I miss
Have we lost a connection?
A connection we needed
I hope to see you soon
On a crowded day
Have we lost a connection?
A connection we needed
I hope to see you soon
On a crowded day
As I've grown happier
The world has grown sadder
Leading me back to where it is cold
Dropping whisky back onto ice
Thoughts back onto a page
I have found myself alone
And there's no one left in Shoreditch
No love within the coke and smoke
Mumbles for a score
We're in a city of monuments
Of what has come before
And I had felt the same inside a room

With each puff of a rock, it's smoke
Before I found you
Those eyes I miss
Have we lost a connection?
A connection we needed
I hope to see you soon
On a crowded day
Have we lost a connection?
A connection we needed
I hope to see you soon
On a crowded day
I'm strolling through Brick Lane
The days that could've been
Arnos Grove and Bermondsey
Memories that come to mind
I'm strolling through Bethnal Green
All I've done and seen
Whitechapel and Hackney
Memories that come to mind
I'm strolling passed The Towers
Through the dead flowers
Islington and Southwark
Memories that come to mind
I'm strolling through St James Park
Through the evening dark
All those places I visited with you
It was beautiful
Have we lost a connection?
A connection we needed
I hope to see you soon
On a crowded day
Have we lost a connection?
A connection we needed
I hope to see you soon
On a crowded day.

Sheena Dell

A 5-7-5 on a strange sort of writer's block

Overwhelm stifles
Words wash each other away
Before I can write.

Tish Camp

Because The Great Tits Have Flown
Written for a friend and in respect of universal grief themes

Because the Great Tits have flown
I am sat without, but you
you knew all along
that they would go
when you brought my tea
when you touched my shoulder
to comfort me.

Now, in this space, we call home
there are no gardens that
could offer solace for
the emptiness that remains
like a vacuum of echoed wings
catching 'flit flit' air
as they danced past me
with their feathered castanets.

Now that the Great Tits have flown,
The newspaper is just a poor replacement
no matter how hard I try
to emulate their 'flit flit' wings
no matter that I pretend
your hand had eased
the 'don't be sad' in me.

Ann-Marie Kurylak

Breathe

Help me breathe
leave this debris and see
that I am still me
and not lost in this
mist
Fading into nothingness
and not a second guess
I am still here
Fight and fire
Climb higher
Reach the top of that spire
and scream into infinity
I am strong
Air, fire, water earth
I've grown from the dirt
bloodied and worn
Skin torn
Releasing my battle cry
to the skies
rending the air
until the clouds are stripped bare
and I will stand
strong and proud
Not beaten down
By my own mind
Or those around
I'll stand my ground and
You will hear the thunder of my voice
The goddess of my soul
Not broken but whole and
here I will be
For eternity
Proud to be me.

Charlie Markwick

Butter Mintoes

Molly loved Butter Mintoes

Butter mintoes pop into my life,
This isn't magic, it's because my darling wife
Loved a butter mintoe more than she loved me.
And sitting in the car to go out she
Would find that lurking creamy minty sweet,
Unwrap it and then proceed to eat.
And as Dementia started to progress,
She would hide them in the pocket of her dress,
Or in perhaps the dressing table drawer,
Or in the magazine rack on the floor.
I once found one she'd wrapped up in a sock,
Another, sticky, dropped behind the clock.
And if asked why she squirrelled them away?
She'd look surprised it "wasn't me" she'd say.
I'd smile and then we'd sit and puzzle why
These pesky little mints would multiply.
Perhaps we said they scuttled round at night,
When the minty little toads were out of sight.
And so it was with oh so many things,
That objects without legs would find their wings.
They'd arrange themselves around our happy home,
With no pretence of logic they would roam.
The enfridged pants, the false teeth in the tea,
The butter on the mat with jam … sticky!
And now she's gone and nothing strays away.
I must divest, an organising sort of day.
I miss her loads but I wear my bravest face.
I'm being ruthless, making book shelf space.
Hmm oddly skewy spines! I take a look,
A butter mintoe has been hidden in a book.

Josephine Lay

Cemented
Maybe not quite fitting Ziggy's brief, in his challenge 20/01/20

Cemented to this bed like
jam on a buttered slice
he sticks, this slothful creature,
courts rest, evades sleep.
Concepts circle in his brain,
ideas as sharp as citrus
a taste of clementine
in his amorphous mental cloud.
Muscles as soft as sponge
he oozes across pillows
eyes like ovens in his face
a mouth of rotting teeth
breathing the stench of offal.

Clive Oseman

Come Together

I'm trying to write
but my mind is in lockdown,
the ideas all two metres apart
(which is a problem
when you're as small minded as me),
and some are sunbathing in the park
illegally,
probably nude.
.

I always did have naughty thoughts.
.

One day they will all come together
(Ooer missus)
have lots of babies
and make a poem.
.

And it won't be a haiku.
Oh no. It will be an epic,
I will let it flow,
become too long for a slam,
full of metaphor and trendy words
like fam.
.

But damn,
it's not happening yet.
The ideas are still not side by side
so, you'll have to make do with this
and be satisfied.

Scott Cowley (aka Rusty Goat)

Darkest Hours ~ First Draft
This is a shorter first draft of the poem that appeared in Scott Cowley's book,
'Not Under My Breath'

Three-oh-Six a.m. and I find myself in this dark cold emptiness, where
not even a mouse is stirring, let alone awake.
All I can hear is the rapidly increasing beat of my heart as my thoughts
flit and skip and the piercing silence of the darkness overrides.

My fragile mind it drip-feeds me what I know to be lies, those
questions, no, those statements that are so loud at this time of night,
chipping away at me one tick of the clock at a time, each tock as loud as
the hours chime.

Memories hitting me full on, point blank two shotgun cartridges are
emptied onto my chest. I take a cutthroat razor to my neck, because it's
true to kill the beast you have to first remove its head.

Three-thirty-Seven a.m. my heart still beats.
And I ask myself; well, how did I get here?

Z. D. Dicks

Demystifying Murder

He walked by the path
scanned loose stone
pressed deep in mud
as he scuffed wet grass

The air congealed
past the door mat
into a curtain wall
of fly perfume

The scent was held
on black lace wings
that hummed a hammer
to eyes, sugar to gut

The world was held
in absent pulse
as he surveyed a scene
two bodies lay
on the carpet twitching

both undressed.

Josephine Lay

Distanced

I've been side lined
left to unwind
to tick tock down
till hands slow.

Shunted into a siding
left to rust
outside of town
where winds blow and
the sands of time
slowly build around me.

One day they'll flow in
and I will stop.

Derek Dohren

Drizzle

Light drizzle falls
from a sky, tar macadam grey
as I advance up the A466.
At the embalmed village of St Weonards
a wooden roadsign informs
and I make mental notes.
234 miles to Lands End
six twenty-nine John O'Groats.
Through Wormelow and Callow
closing in on Hereford now
this drizzle drenched drive.
Picking up speed on the A49
I finally arrive.
On the Ross Road
a pre-pubescent boy
out playing on his bike
gives me a wanker sign.
I feel affronted
until I remember
that my generation will hand over
a completely fucked up planet
to his generation
and I think
'yeah ok then, fair enough'.
It continues to drizzle lightly
as I cruise over the Old Bridge
but I cannot quite find
the right frequency of swipe
for my windscreen wipers
and I don't know what to do.
They are either swiping too much
or the swipes are too few.
Then I see him on the corner

of Saint Martins and Wye
breaking cover momentarily
from the fancy dress shop doorway
where he'd sheltered, unironically
Bus Spotter Man
his plumage adapted to the season
pallid and wan.
His cavernous winter coat designed
to conceal flasks of Bovril
and packets of Dundee cake.
I skirt carefully by
but out shoots a telescopic lens
a co-ordinated flurry of arms and fingers
and I know I'm snapped
as a fly by a frog.
Before he slinks back to the concrete
I sneak a second glance.
Cowboy boots upon his feet
torn and shredded pants.
I've not seen this one before
probably blown off course by the weather
so, I make a new entry and tick him off
in my notebook.
And still the drizzle falls.
At the station animated football fans
congregate menacingly.
Stockport County are in town
and hooded youths take turns
to goad one another
while disinterested police officers
stare at their mobile phones.
I offer up a fervent plea
'Please don't any of you
even think about getting on'.
The second I am able to
I pull the bus away
devoid of passengers
through the clag filled traffic spray

to make my way to Monmouth.
I trade waves with a fellow driver
acknowledging the camaraderie
of the shared experience
though my bus is bigger than his
and this makes me feel superior
but only for the briefest of moments
before it makes me feel foolish.
On the Ross Road
I see Wanker Boy again
still out with his mates
playing on his bike.
They don't seem to care
what the weather's like
and I want to tell them
those friendships forged
when you're only ten
you're unlikely to ever see
the like of them again.
And at last the weather concurs
that enough is surely enough
and so the change occurs
I'm in the A49 bus lane
when drizzle finally turns
into cathartic full-blown rain.

Emma Lord

Dust to Dust

Capped by silver crowns
Which glisten
Beneath the gentle caress
Of springtime sun beams
The mountains bear witness.
We are gathered here today
Three generations strong
To say farewell.
Easing the lids off small wooden barrels
And facing away from the wind
We take turns
To release dust
to dust.
Caught momentarily
By the breeze which tumbles across the mountainside
We soon lose sight of the ashes
As they are swept away
To rest.
The barrels empty,
We stand a while
Staring without seeing
Each in our own thoughts
Until, turning silently together
As though directed by an unseen hand
We leave
Nobody else saw
But the mountains
Wearing their crowns of silver.

Derek Dohren

Eleven ~ First Draft

Tossed from the Tower of Babel
in statuesque silence
I lay there unobserved
in splendid splendour
a flown-out reverie
ampersand underscore asterisk dot com.
Impressing the ladies
with my street magic
it seems there are some things
I can do that God can't.
I don't require
anyone on their knees
praising me for all eternity
for example
But I was thinking more about
sinning and dying
and coming in at number eleven
in someone's all-time top ten list.
Lost at the Battle of Culloden
not a hint of motion
I lay there unobserved
in flagrant vagrancy
a grown-out topiary
ampersand underscore asterisk dot com.
The prophetic Messiah
a lingering trespasser
it seems there are some things
I can do that God can't.
I don't require
endlessly trying to wash away
the fluff on a new set of towels
for example
But I was thinking more about

lying there unobserved
and coming in at number eleven
in someone's all-time top ten list.

May need editing but I want to say it now.

Simon Alderwick

Everyone Gets 15 Minutes

our universe, filled with ironies
like the missus
who only listens to love songs
when she hates you
and that great poet
who said it's love
that holds the stars apart
when even a blind fool can see
it's nothing
that keeps the stars apart
in fact, 99% of the universe
is empty space
and the other 1%
is all kinds of emotions
so, I won't tell you how to feel
about the apparent successes
and apparent failures
'cos "there's no success like failure
and failure's no success at all"
played on the radio
as the waiter welcomed me to
the centre of the universe
I said "how do you figure?"
and he told me
the Milky Way is the centre of the universe
Earth is the centre of the Milky Way
Europe is the centre of Earth
Austria is the centre of Europe
Vienna is the centre of Austria
and where I was sat was bang in the centre of Vienna
I figured it made about as much
sense as anything
enjoyed my 15 minutes and a coffee

then was on my way
pulled by forces
beyond comprehension.

JLM Morton

Figure of Speech
Waterland Poet in Residence 2020 - March

I met a jack pike
gravel studded and alive
jack-knifing on the path.

Eye big as breakfast fish
eyes on Chinese trains, bloodless,
a serrated surface wound.

I knelt to hold it, tenderly
as a friend   it held me
and we slipped through the post-dawn dull,

cloudwards, precise as infantry,
chanting – must we take our place?
Our gills flaring red fires.

Jason Conway

Five Valleys Delight

I've finally got round to this 1st Draft, in response to Ziggy's poetry challenge on the 20th January. For those that didn't read it, the task was to write a poem about where you are as a place but to describe it as a person, a person made of food. My place is Stroud, Gloucestershire

She is a rebellious dish with a smile that beams like clementine
Peel back her folds and be soaked in the nectar of rich culture
Her vibrant sprinkles adorn a fancy, trinkets glittering a treasure
Sherry steeped foundations perfectly balance contrasting notes
Custard supple skin, firmed and cracked from defiant rally cries
She has known many battles, troops hungered, deftly filled with fanfares
Cream whipped festive clouds, snugly float over a fruitful community
Her swaying sponge base, playfully bobs with shifts in gravity
She is a dreamy dessert, a decadent dish in the Cotswolds

This honeyed siren weathers ravaging teeth, lips licked dry
Unsavoury mouths may prefer offal but she has a modicum of taste
Offal is for those with poor diets and plain caked conversations
There is an honesty to her flavour, filled by nature's garden
Her future rests in the happiest of bellies, comforted, wholesome
She has a memory that lingers in the driest palate, kaleidoscopic in death
Gracing this world, carefree, independent, a widely respected delicacy
Blessing local tables with a perfectly delicious blend of community life

But each day I devour her, savour her, each swallow caressed, indulged
I love her eclectic, soft contrasts as her name dances in my hot breath
My tongue is left wet, her masterpiece painted in luscious delights
My nights are sugared by silken textures and graceful slopes
Her vibrance spikes my blood as I crave her smoothly pressed folds
Tomorrow, my appetite for her plentiful gifts will race once more
As she treats my eager hunger with the sweetest pleasures of life.

Kuma San

Forget Me Not 2

I had the privilege of reading this at Raised Voices yesterday... thank you all 🖤

I am the voiceless
Watching my children die hungry…
Knowing that other people dream but forgetting why.

I am the besieged,
hoping that my heart beat is enough life for the child swaddled in my
arms...as the world around me detonates.

I am the stolen
Used, discarded, punished.
Adrift in a parallel universe...
only touching your world when it hits or kills me.

I am the battered and abused…
Silently suffering till death us do part.

Forget me not...
Remember me....my breathing softness.

Celebrate my life as a woman,
A sister who danced on this earth....
One familiar with your journey as you are with hers.

Remember that I loved and was loved in return...
That like you, I dreamed and held hope close on the darkest nights.

Remember that the ripples of my fate, inevitably shape your life.

Dance for me...remember who you are!

Forget me not.

Josephine Lay

For I Am A Coward
Unedited first version

For I am a coward
running from images of horror;
children in poverty, hungry, crying,
cowering as kicked dogs.
Women trapped like birds
behind the cages of front doors.

People dying alone in aseptic tents
hands grasping gloved fingers.
Carers sweating, exhausted, scared.

But I am a coward and dive
into the soft green of spring
into the endless blue of sky
as I drown in birdsong.

For I am a coward
powerless and angry,
lost and confused like the world.

For I am a coward seeking survival
fleeing into nature and narrative
suckling on the teats of creation
in the hope she will feed me.

Charlie Markwick

Frankie's

In Brae we'd booked a table
A chip shop, the most northern one
They claim.
We've just driven through
The beauty of sea and sun and voe.
And stopped to eat.
Stepping in we meet unexpected friends
Some we've known for many many years
Another met first the other day on Lerwick's quay.
I sit with monk's fish tails delicious
Deep fried in Panko
The home-made Tartar Sauce is sharp
A harmony to squeezing lemon note,
Dripped across the fish.
Through glass
The hills round Olnafirth
Are silhouetted by the sinking
Northern sun.
So perfect in every way.
Except.
I watch the couple on the seats outside
Enjoying view, enjoying scrumptious
Fish and chips like us as well.
Then she rests her head against his arm.
The devastation swamps my heart.
She used to nestle to me in that way.
The challenge of rising through the pain
Is never far away.
It's that that hurts
Again, again, again, again.

Stephen Moore

Greta

A local radio presenter made light of Greta Thunberg's campaigning and I was seething. How can anyone not admire the work of someone who seeks to allow our children some chance of growing and surviving?

A girl steps up to save this world from itself

and shells fly from the pens of cynics.

Blunt rocks,

thrown at glass,

land at the feet of their own children's greenhouses.

Matty Blades

Hand in Hand

The night we walked hand in hand
The moon hung bright and low
We vowed that night
We'd be together forever
And for you I suppose that was true
Our hearts entwined throughout the night
Blissfully sharing our spirits
Your pagan beliefs washed over me
Loyal, loving and giving
You were so much more than my partner
You were my best friend
My soul mate carried off into the ether
Our energy never ends
I feel you here from time to time
Into my mind with that precious smile
All the while, eyes like diamonds
Compassionate, warm and inviting.

Devlin Wilson

Hegira

As I wandered through the desert
I came across a man fashioning coffins.
He said to me:
'It would be all too easy to speak
In sweeping and grandiose statements,
To insist the world is changed, changed utterly
And nothing will ever be the same.
Yet as the dust settles
Collective amnesia will kick in
And the old reflexes will assert themselves,
Even as the black flowers of forgetting
Bloom from the scorched earth.
Your lived experience is unique but unremarkable.
The game has changed, and the challenge now
Will be to start anew in a different place and time.'
The man turned and walked away,
Quickly vanishing amongst his catafalques.
I retraced my steps towards the city,
Casting a trail of ghostly footprints
In the white sand.
Ahead, carrion birds banked and wheeled
Between the phone masts
And the prayerful were summoned
To distant minarets.
Hello cruel world;
I kiss you on the mouth.

Nick Lovell

Her at Number 10

Theresa
Brexit teaser
Budget squeezer
Born deceiver
DUP appeaser
Was remainer
Now a leaver
Just can't believe her
Not Theresa

Prime minister
Slightly sinister
Smile like vinegar
Eyes are similar
Not a listener
When she goes
No one missing her
Clings to Westminister
Our Prime Minister

Negotiations
Insulted nations
British impatience
Insane expectations
Unforgivable complacence
Broken promises
To the population
Divided nation
Negotiations

Brexit
Boris wrecked it
Bigots expect it

Lots reject it
Can't correct it
Self-destruct kit
Bottomless pit
No way
To fix it
Can't respect it
Stupid Brexit.

Drea MacMillan

He Was Warmth

você me fez sorrir de novo, eu nunca vou te esquecer, sempre em meu coração

A layer of sunburst lacquer, glowing
burnt sienna, crimson and gloss
radiating light
He was red
A juicy dark cherry toasted in the sun
skin glossy, taut and hers
so sweet
He was spice
Heady sandalwood musk and cloves
Smouldering incense, a fragrant
amber haze
He was wildfire
An uncontainable, uncontrollable fever
blazing frenzied sparks like
shooting stars
He was heat
A solid brick buried deep in the fire hearth
Searing her body, with his
Burning embers
She was frozen
Breathing plumes of icy snowflakes
His fervour thawed her slowly
She melted.

Jason Conway

Hibernating
a poem inspired by a line from WH Auden's 'Funeral Blues' (Stop all the clocks)
and a line by Emily Dickenson

Face swollen, patterned with grit and blood
My hands scraped raw, pith from peel
Limbs twisted, heavy like soaked timbers
Chest flat, breath slow like damp fire
Vision black, flashed by random sparks
The numbness of impact, cold, hibernating

A crowd gather, curious like foxes
Nudging a mannequin, left stringless
Air rushed to lungs like sponge to water
Eyes twitched, focus regained, a smile curled
'Because I could not stop for death
He kindly stopped for me.'

Alby Stockley

Home Ruin

Sometimes I miss that sacred madness
The safety of
That thread worn home ruin
Where jam is smeared
Beans dry hard shrivelled
Old toast lies cold
On piled up plates
Where sounds and shouts
Fall always on
That deaf tuned ear
Where wars are fought with
Home made chips and Lego wands
Where tears and angry screams
Turn to vendettas and 'they're on my side' teams
Who swap sides at will or with the enticement of your marbles stash.
Before interlopers come in between
In which case we are now all on the same team
Don't think you can ever come in between
That sacred safety
Of that peeling wall paper home ruin
Where spilt squash dries sticky on the side
Where we argue over whose turn is it to dry
Shout it was an accident the towel flick caught you in the eye.
Mumble cry baby as Ma storms in
Face like you best not answer back
And one of us ends up crying on the bottom step
Where favourite things are gleefully hidden
Until action man's all-terrain vehicle is held to ransom
Where we hate as intensely as we love
Where we forget most but not all misdemeanours
'Cos some we keep as parting shots
Or store for ammo in future wars
Like who was last to feed the rabbit and left the cage door open

Or who drew on the spot the ball ticket
Or who nicked the biscuits from Ma's not very secret, secret cashe
Or who hides their cigarettes under the fir tree in the front garden
Or who broke the back door window
Or who drank the Cinzano
Sometimes I miss the safety of the don't open that window the wood's
rotten home ruin
But then mostly it just remains unmentioned
Like a testament of survival
Where hurts run in underground rivers
Where the tearing of seams echo in caverns
And the fruits from the trees that didn't survive the lightning
Roll down the hills in different directions.

Kuma San

Hope

The sun rose this morning
Casting clouds in regal hues
Spilling light on frosty ground...
Unhurried without bias its breath
warmed the back of passing wind.
Flowers nodded....
wise heads turning to follow its trajectory.
Birds wove their soundscape in to the rising day.
The grip of ice loosed....released to sun glazed earth.
While we worry about dying
daylight has broken the dark!

Drea MacMillan

Hyacinthoides Non-Scripta

Playing with (westernised) Haikus after a walk yesterday and feeling inspired after Ziggy's workshop last week. Each stanza should be able to be read separately, yet also as a whole. I love the history behind flowers.

A flood of blue grief.
Mythical flowers emerge
from metallic soil

Apollo's tears fell.
Petals enscribed with 'alas'
mark spilt blood, lost love

Stems of blue vessels.
Upended fragile glass flutes.
Nought to celebrate.

Above, hand sized leaves
protect my head from raindrops
Yet my cheeks are wet

My lover has gone.
Absorbed by the winter soil.
I sit here and weep.

Amidst the bluebells
an albino stalk wails.
Alone in a crowd.

.

Devlin Wilson

If I'm Spared

If I'm spared
I will become a post-trauma calliope
Singing for sanctuary
In impromptu isolation wards
If I'm spared
I will transform field hospitals
Into free festivals
As open air epicentres
Of elaborate skylarking
If I'm spared
I will etch the history of the crisis
On earthenware amphorae
With ponderous cuneiform.

Darryl John

Infinity

tick, tick
time won't stop
sixty seconds you can't spare
grains of sand that slip
through our hands get washed away
or are swept away like dust
seconds, minutes, hours, are spent
bartered and taken.
From that first cry to decaying memories
flows endlessly only changing pace.
No heart or pulse, but is alive,
from wrist to wall
has no master yet serves all.

Chris Barber

In My Own Skin

Zonally uncomfortable, imposter, someone will discover soon, I know
it, though they haven't yet, I feel the hot breath of self-loathing get
closer, no matter how harder I try, how faster I run, the hunt is never
over, I can't escape me.
Feeling love is undeserved, from people I'll never match, too self-
absorbed, too racked with doubt to look without.
Eyes lifted, mouth opened, secret fears made known. Oh, you too.

Morgan 'I'm-not-a-poet' Rye

I Think of You, Unprotected

I think of you
unprotected,
managed by a power
without care.
I think of you,
long hours,
desperate people,
empty shelves.
I worry for you,
a mother's fear,
the worst of all,
and shut it away.
I admire you,
my baby,
standing the line,
fierce.
I miss you,
my chest aches,
my eyes burn,
and talk myself to belief.
Because I need you,
to stay healthy,
to live life,
to set my ashes free.

Chris Barber posted

Jobs, For What They're Worth

Do your homework,
or you'll wind up sweeping
streets, study hard, or your
future lies in the collection
of refuse, learn a trade,
get ahead, earn pieces
of paper, play the game,
but only to win.
Start of a working week.
Stan the shithouse cleaner,
never missed a day, dozen
years or more, poorly, can't
come in today.
Managing Director is ill too.
Everyone noticed Stan wasn't in.

Derek Dohren

John O'Groats
Based on a weird dream I had and (sort of) put into poetry...

I had a dream I was in Lands End
and I met a Scotsman who became my friend
He said his name was John O'Groats
and he'd travelled all the way by boat
"What, from John O'Groats?", I asked
"No, from Truro.
John O'Groats is just my name."
"Well", I said, "still, it's a co-incidence
all the same."
"What is?" said John O'Groats.
"That you're called John O'Groats
and now you're here in Lands End", I said
"Oh, I haven't really thought about it", said John O'Groats
Then we started singing 'Do They Know It's Christmas'
for it was November.
"I remember hearing this song last November too", I said.
"What a coincidence", said John O'Groats.
In an attempt to change tack I said
"I've been to John O'Groats."
"What's John O'Groats like then?" asked John O'Groats
"It's the kind of place people are either
dying to see or dying to get away from", I said.
"Now, that is a coincidence", said John O'Groats.
"What is?", I asked
"That people are either dying to see John O'Groats
or dying to get away from John O'Groats,
just like they are with you", replied John O'Groats.
"Are they?", I asked
"Yes", said John O'Groats.
"How do you know?", I asked.
"Because I'm one of them aren't I", said John O'Groats.
Then we started a fresh version of 'Do They Know It's Christmas'

for it was even more November.

"I remember singing this song a few minutes ago", said John O'Groats.

"What a coincidence", I said.

In an attempt to change tack, John O'Groats asked

"Why are you in Lands End then?"

"I dunno. It's just a dream isn't it.

This is where the dream started off", I said.

"It's not a dream to me", said John O'Groats.

"I'm real.

I've got a back story and everything."

"Have you always lived in Truro then?" I asked.

"No, I've never lived in Truro", said John O'Groats.

"I live in Sheffield.

"I just sailed here from Truro".

"Oh", I said

"What a coincidence".

"What is?" said John O'Groats

"I don't know", I said

"I haven't really thought about it."

Carol Sheppard

Journey
inspired by W S Merwin's Travelling Together

If we become separated, I
will wait for you by the railway track, in case
you choose to follow the rusted rails, jumping
from one blackened sleeper to another as you go.
I will dispense dry leaves to fly like moths to find you, send
a smoke signal from a dirty diesel engine high
to mix with the peppermint clouds, startle
flocks of resting rooks hunkered in the trees
so they take flight, scatter like splashed ink.
I will sail flotillas of paper boats down the rivers
and shoot fireworks into the night sky.

So that wherever you are
you will see and know that I am close.

Chloë Jacquet

Keep Shit Simple
For National Writing Day

Do not think that poetry
necessitates grandiose vocabulary.
Be not ensnared in grandiloquence
or ostentatious phraseology.
Circumlocute extraneous intricacy.
Synthesise your assertion succinctly.
Postulate your doctrine in an epigrammatic consuetude.
There is aught misguided in sustaining
feculence unencumbered.

Charlie Markwick

Life Sentence
A poem for International Women's Day

She sat head bowed,
Children clutching at her hands
Shaking crying as she braved her fear.
"He'll kill me if he knows I'm here" she says
We make her tea. The smell of toast
Gives brief respite.
And as I talk she cocks her head
So my words fall upon her good ear
The other deaf from blows.
More floods of tears
Recriminations of herself.
Molly kneels in front,
Wraps her arms around her life.
I gather two girls and boy
We snuggle on the floor
I read a book and sing them songs.
Two weeks later she goes home
She hopes he's changed.
He hasn't.
Then more years of broken bones
Fleeing back to us
And fleeing back to him.
Then one day a call
She says she's standing firm
Divorcing him.
We've heard it all before of course
Still we treat this like the first.
But this is the one.
Resolve has risen from the
Violence in her life.
She rings to say
She's now a nisi wife.

Divorce day dawns,
We gather at the court
And she is absolutely firm.
He stumbles out of court
Red faced and angry
That his hold has gone.
Except
As we gather on the street
He turns and walks two steps
And dies. The heart he never had
Has stopped.
And in that moment guilt returns,
The children blame her for his death
No court can free her now.

Brian Reid

Lockdown

You can't see it til it's in you
You can't feel it til it hits you
You can't dodge it when it surrounds you
You can't engage safe mode
Your walking blindfold in the middle of the road
Unsure and scared soon to be permanently scarred
A global levelling event
This is gold medal content
Nothing will ever be the same again
Whatever you think reality is just changed
The musics out of sync
Not matter what you think
All the hand wringing in the world is too little and much too late
Global economics about to stagnate and no amount of spin can help us relate
Everything is built on the lie of stability
But life is full of volatility
Seething raging flaring and glaring
Violence just below the surface
Ready for deep sharing
The dragons within us unleashed by fear and power cuts
Be fearful,
be tearful
be grateful
Don't let bravado and ignorance make you hateful

Chris Barber

Loss
In Memoriam, Roy Barber 1935 to 2020.

He held my hand, tightly,
I'm sure that had happened
before, but I don't remember.
Felt this sadness before,
long enough ago to have
forgotten, now it's too familiar.
Can't think what to say, say
nothing, the contact is enough.
Now I think of what I'll miss.
Everything, even the withering
piss takes, razor sharp wit
disguising the kindness.
Two words.
He cared.
That's
what people said when I
delivered the news.

Proud.

Vicky Hampton

Lottie
'Out flew the web, and floated wide'

So, Knight and burgher, lord and dame
by the wharfage, where they'd come,
gasped to find the lady - not dead, as some
had said, but looking wanly on
      at the faces here at Camelot.
But, minstrel, maid, reaper, jest,
laughed as royalty crossed its chest;
they knew their own kind from the rest;
      this *lady* of Shalott!

"Oh, get over yourselves", they cried.
"Tis only Lottie with her over-plied
endeavours to be Lancelot's bride.
How many times has she tried
      now, coming into Camelot?!"
"I'm *not* Lottie" the wee girl stamped
on getting up, unfolding cramped
and aching limbs. "I'm the re-vamped
      Lady of Shalott."

The crowd guffawed and then dispersed,
and Lottie felt the mirror's curse
had more to do with life than first
she'd thought. "I know, I'll put them into verse
      and send up all at Camelot."
Resolved, she stepped out from her boat
and, turning, saw Sir Lancelot gloat
(while flicking his finger across his throat)
      at the Lady of Shalott.

"Huh" she scoffed. "I'm well relieved.
For all your plumes and brazen greaves,

up close, you're like rained-on barley-sheaves.
You've more drip than willow leaves
        on the way down to Camelot".
High-horsed Lancelot, seeing his cover blown,
offered his hand to help her down,
thinking he ought to have earlier known
        this Lady of Shalott.

Refusing, she gave him a withering look.
 "Tirra lirra? Pff! time I forsook
that notion of romance", and her Book
of Knights she chucked into the clogged-up brook
        outside the gates Camelot.
She found a pub within the city,
had several beers, and, sitting to write her ditty,
stuck two fingers to the sleazeballs with their "Oh, *pretty*
        Lady of Shalott".

Her writing made her mildly famous.
She matured on Keates and Camus,
and from romanticism's stale hiatus
grew a woman who recognised ignoramus
        in the high offices of Camelot.
She settled among the poor but worthy,
wrote when she wanted, drank when thirsty,
and befriended those who called her 'that wordy
        lady from Shalott'.

As time went on the island faded.
The tower, her stitching, and all those jaded
knights of yore just degraded –
this lass preferred the un-pomaded,
        bawdy Camelot.
She married the reaper who'd listened, teary,
all those years back among the barley,
and was never happier when, coitus-weary,
        he'd beam, gasping, "Lady, that's your lot!"

Drea MacMillan

Love is Not

Love is not something you
                                fall
                                    into
No, love is something you choose to pick up
Your love, a piece of glass shimmering on a black beach
caught the only ray of sun
                thrown
                      below
through tempestuous charcoal skies
pissing down rain and vicious biting winds

A flash of bright bottle green on dusty black ash
you caught my eye in the darkest weather
Finding love amidst a storm is never a good idea
I chose to pick you up and treasure you
To wrap my fingers tightly around your changing edges
But my fingers started to bleed beneath my desperate grasp
and I blemished your beauty, dulled your shine
I should put
                You
                    Back
                        Down
Sometimes it hurts too much to hold on to love.

Jason Conway

Love Isn't

Thought I'd share this poem written two years ago, ☺
as right now, the world needs a little love! Happy Valentines...

Love isn't the gifts you get
it's the prickles on the back of your neck
love isn't the priciest food you've tried
it's the joyful feast you both share inside
love isn't about the car they drive
it's the journey beyond the stars in their eyes
love isn't the words they want to hear
it's the warmth of your lips that speak so clear
love isn't a parade of who spent most
it's falling freely, being blissfully lost
love isn't a prize to hoard in banks
it's sharing the richness of life with thanks
love isn't the expectations of others
it's openly loving without any cares
love isn't something to hide
it's for sharing here and spreading wide
love isn't meant just for two
it's for sending across this world of blue
love isn't something to be bought
it's your gift to care and lend support
love isn't a part-time thing
it's absorbing the joy of everything
love isn't to be expected
it's given freely from heart and head
love isn't hidden in a place so rare
it's in open eyes for you to stare
love isn't lost to fleeting lust
it's a bond we weave in open trust
love isn't priced on high street shelves
It's free to all in natures wealth
love isn't synthetic, a man-made thing

it's the dance of light on feathered wings
love isn't a puzzle without a key
it's simply the knowing that I is we.

Dave Seed

Megaloceros Giganteus of the Tribe Megacerini

King of the deer
once ranged from the bogs of Ballybetagh
to abysmal Lake Baikul.
You grazed the wooded steppes
where tundra turned to bosk.
A narrow band between
the bears and pachyderms,
and Southern monkeys
with their sharpened sticks and fire.
Two great trees grown from your skull
dead oaks rattling
in the rut
Such hungry work.
Antlers feeding on your bones,
springtime osteoporosis,
and a need for lime-rich fodder.
You had enough velvet for a king's wardrobe.
The monkeys drew you in soot and ochre,
rubbing your spirit into the walls at Lascaux
whilst mining your continents of flesh
Peat cutters found your sheddings
root stump ploughshares
scapulas like shovel blades
And named you Fiaghmore,
Schelch and Segh
We see you
washed clean and wired,
vertebral picket fence and leafspring legs
Labelled and lit
extinct exhibit,
fire monkeys still rubbing your spirit into the walls.
Cernunnos is belling yet.

Jonathan Robert Muirhead

Mona Lisa
Previously entitled: POEM - SO SAD IN SAINSBURYS - DRAFT 1

Your face to me
This morning was
Like the Mona Lisa
Dissolving slowly

It seemed to drip
Onto the heel of
Your hand
And your wrist

All white
Around the veins
Seemed to sparkle
With melancholy

The shop lights painted
Circles of pale white
And yellow around you
A small halo of sadness

And all around you
The buzz and drone
Of folk and families
All panic buying

No one saw you
Apart from me
Once I'd seen your eyes
I could not look away

Small wells of emotion
That seemed to
Slowly get bigger
The longer I looked

So I did not
Look too long
But yet not long enough
To know you a moment

I wanted to
Speak to you
But did not dare
Lest I upset you further

How, I don't know
But I felt
For you still
Why, I know not

But I felt for you still
There, on your own
Or at least that's
How you seemed

At that moment
At that time
In this shop
In this town

Maybe because
You could not get
All the goods
That you needed

Maybe because
You weren't feeling well
Or maybe because
You weren't feeling at all

I don't know
I didn't ask
It didn't feel right
But I hope you're ok now.

Lucia Daramus

Music of All Languages
because I am a European ...

I am from the East and South and North
when the wind dances so, so slowly
and is singing the story of its people
the fields, like in England, are green and shaggy
the clouds are whirling on the sky
and the sky is so, so fragile and blue
like my soul which is keeping entire planet
But you, you don't understand this
because of your inner deconstruction's revolution
mister, mister Boris Johnson
I am just a woman
staying in front of a strong man
what can I do, what can I do, what can I do?
my powers are only my words! Words, words, words
what can I do, what can I do? What can I do?!
On the streets there are many conflicts
a special culture fights against another one
everywhere is a fight, yes a fight!
Mister Boris Johnson
I am not a terrorist, I am a European
domnule Boris Johnson, nu sunt o terorista
sunt o europeana
Señor Boris Johnson, no soy un terrorista soy un europeo
Signore, io non sono un terrorista, io sono un europeo
Κύριε, δεν είμαι τρομοκρατής είμαι Ευρωπαίος
I am from The East, and South and North
when lambs are jumping with happiness
and peasants knead ancestral clay
with their hands, worked hands.
The door of their soul is open
for each human ! - because
my country is Romania

when Brancusi crushed the stones
to make his Golden Bird to fly over the world
my country is Poland
when Chopin touched with his
fragile fingers the sounds of our nature
my country is Germany, and England, and Italy, and Spain
Spain, Spain, Spain when Picasso
and Salvador Dali painted
my country is Denmark, and Greece
and, and, and....
because I am a Muslim
Buddhist
Jew
Muslim
Christian
yes, mister Boris Johnson
I am a European, I am a European
and in my veins is flowing
the music of all languages!

Kuma San

My Feet Rest

My feet rest on cropped turf
Legs heavy with climbing.
Around me granite bones of the leviathan hill break through the moss,
Gorse bushes lie twisted and folded crone like by the winds urgent
passage.
Ears ring
Eyes whipped to tears.
Silent breath heaves at my chest…
Upward eyes find the clouds...
At the top of the world I am given the sky.

Annalisa Jackson

Ode to a Cheese Toastie

Perfect
Imperfect
Why strive to be one and run from the other. Why assume they aren't actually sister and brother?
Maybe they aren't poles on a map or a bad bipolar joke. Maybe they spring from the same well.
Maybe they serve a common need.
Why assume everyone has to have a goal or a purpose?
Maybe I will have a porpoise. One of the ones trained by a call centre using the data they collected.
Then embrace my perfectly warped and eccentric self.
And growl at anybody who steals one of the few jokes I came up with myself even if it will have been made before by someone with a perfect gift for comedy
And not just someone who likes making people laugh then groan
Like me
I'm fed up of worrying about who I'm meant to be and just want to be who I need to be.
Imperfect.
Sitting here browsing Amazon for toasters for the simple reason I've decided my kitchen needs to be duck egg blue not red, a whole other issue I realise I'm content with my life right now as it is.
Red toaster being the possible exception.
And my Amazon bill
But
I've spent a long time learning
It's OK to just be ok
And that's not me celebrating mediocrity
Because you should be the best you, you could be
Except... What if your best you is just you being happy?
I've written about the drudgery of chasing unattainable perfection in my past career because I realised I don't need to be the best nurse ever to have contributed.

If everybody was the best nurse to have ever been then nobody would have been the best nurse to have ever been.
And that's just sad
Because for every best person
There are a million just doing their best
Changing the world one imperfect being at a time
I contribute by being my best me and if my best me is the best nurse ever well that's just great
But not everyone can be Florence Nightingale
Blazing a pioneering medical trail
And not everyone can turn up to the mic and be John Cooper Clark
And some days I can't write about the wind and the sweetly curving lark
Because all I can think about is cheese
And how there's poetry in a nice cheese toastie. Where the edges meet in a light brown crisp in two perfect triangles with a buttery soft centre bread disguising the yellow stuff of the gods within.
And I wonder how I will ever be the best spoken word poet in the world if I stop halfway to discuss the perfect cheese toastie. And how it doesn't have to try to be the best cheese toastie in the world. Just grab its cheese and it's bread and butter and I will probably love it anyway. Cheese toasties are unfettered by such concerns.
...
I bet Neil Holborn never interrupts his performance to muse on the philosophical leanings of a cheese toastie.
And you know what
That's. OK. Too.
Because I'm not him...
Or Flo...
My photographers eye isn't the best
No David Bailey I guess
Because much as its worth striving to be your best, perfection isn't a destination.
It's the journey. And it comes in a million different forms. Many involving cheese.

I can lie awake at night
Ignoring the snoring on my right

And the urge to punch him in the face

This man I let into my life 15 years ago. And not feel bad for the thoughts of mariticide

Fuelled by the noise closely resembling a 60 a day smoking warthog with a cold

Because I don't have the perfect relationship with this man

And nothing in our life has ever gone to plan. He and I aren't perfect for each other.

You can't really be perfect for somebody you call a twat on a regular basis. Or want to punch in the face a lot

But I don't do it and that's part of my charm. The whole do no harm

Got. It. Nailed.

...

Physically

But he and I. Well, we are imperfect for each other. His imperfections and mine form an intersecting path that always leads to our home. An imperfect spot in an imperfect world. In an imperfect time.

So I'm not going to chase the unattainable perfection. I'm going to embrace this poem that can't even remember when to rhyme and when it's just wasting my time

By bringing me repeatedly back to cheese

And instead learn to be the best me I can be by just being me.

And if it turns out I'm good at something well that's just peachy.

Until then I don't even want to fret if I'm good enough.

I just want to be good

I just want to be enough

And I will work on those until I'm imperfect at them.

Morgan 'I'm-not-a Poet' Rye

Ode to an Aspirational Lay

Floppy of chin and nylon shirt,
You dismissed my glittery pose,
Because I had no PhD,
Just a glass of fizzy rose.

The weight of all is questionable,
Dark matter, you insisted,
My rejection of this line of thought,
You instantly resisted.

Because I wore a powdered face,
Or sported a vagina?
Because I held no papers framed,
To qualify my meander?

A force much like gravity,
An energy, if you will,
Could account for the weight of everything,
In space between its fill.

I see what you're saying but no,
Of course, you are not right,
It is impossible, you proclaimed,
You lack in numbered sight.

What a git you are, I thought,
And let the matter go,
Your unwillingness to debate,
Was a turn-off don't you know.

Twenty years came and went,
And then came the news,
Matter was under scrutiny,
Dark energy now the muse.

Where are you now professor?
Valleys or mountains high?
If only I could find you,
To poke you in the eye.

Sally Aspden

Of Magpies and Spirit

Out of that windswept winter's day
you staggered flightless.

We gave you refuge,
you repaid with curiosity:
I straightened the kitchen, warmed in
company of bright dark eyes
watching entranced.

You taught determination,
launching over and over
into would-be flight.

When the sanctuary took you
they reassured me with
cheerful reports of your
escape attempt. I saw
your spirit still blazed bright.

Trevor Valentine

'One Soul'

We were
At the beginning of time
Perhaps a little before
Together
Not lovers
But one soul
Together
Complete

And then God
Or someone
Or something
Perhaps a devil
Put us apart
And we were left alone
Yearning

Yearning
For how it was
As one soul
Together
Complete

Was that a woeful day
Or just a challenge
To make us
And our children
The stronger for striving
Striving to be as one
Together again
One soul
One special soul
Together

I do not know

For now,
With outward differences
We are marked
And caged
Like animals apart
Looking through bars
Looking for keys
To unlock this damned door
And return
To where we were
Together
Complete
As one

And when I meet
With your mind
Or with your body
Or with both
It is the closest
We can be
The closest
We are allowed to be
Together
But not quite complete

For it is only passing
Momentary
Fleeting
A small instance in time
Of the door being unlocked
For the cursed jailer
Stands by
Rattling the keys
And we must return
To being alone
And incomplete

In my thoughts
In my head

And in my mind
We are as one
And that may be love
Or its definition
The striving
And yearning
To be together again
As one soul

And forgive me
If I would cast away
This frame
This shackle
This cage
These markings
This form
For it is no more befitting me
Than it befits you

And if I am fluid in this
In my mind
In my body
It is not a statement
Or a challenge
It is just
Well, it is just
What is inside
A search for comfort
For inward peace
A tranquillity
A quest for one soul

I am not alone now
I know there are others
Many more who understand
Who seem allowed to understand
And now seek out
Despite or because of our God
The same unfulfilled transition

Forward or back
It matters not
It is fluid

We will stand together
One paternity
One fraternity
One indifference
One unity
One soul.

David Seed

On the perils of a heavily carnivorous diet, and the complications that can arise when there is no meat in the larder

Was on the day the goose had flown
The whole brigade in disarray
The chef, the sous, the confiseur
Knew that the King would make them pay
The feast was due that very night
They had no beast, no fatted calf
No suckling pig or sweet spring lamb,
No zebra plump or small giraffe
They had, it's true, a clamp of spuds
Fresh chard and peas, tomatoes red
Of stock they had eight gallon made
And herbs and greens and fresh made bread
But what to cook for the main meal
For fat King John preferred a roast
He wouldn't stand for lentil stew
Or spinach pie or even toast
The grillardin he had a plan
Thirteen vanilla pods he took
He broke one short and they drew lots
The loser was the one they'd cook
The marmiton and the potager
The garde-manger and rôtisseur
The chef and sous they all drew long
The short pod went to the plongeur
A stocky boy running to fat
He stood there dumb and white with shock
He wrung his hands then cried and yelled
They led him to the butcher's block
Later (considerably later):
And then the hall doors opened wide
A minstrel with a pipe and drum
Strode through the room a herald of

The fine repast that was to come
Six kitchen staff in toques and whites
Walked three in line and two abreast
And in a dish they held aloft
Their brother to be laid to rest
Stop gobbered with an apple plucked
That morning from a cankered tree
All basted with a marinade
And trussed up tidy, elbow to knee
The moral of this little tale
If moral there is to relate
Is if a lot is to be drawn
Then don't walk blindly to you.

Ann-Marie Kurylak

Open Scars
When you have that kind of talk with someone who gets it

Old wounds
Like old friends
Always there and never far from your mind
Take you back to a time
When something tore at your skin
Scratch, ripped and pushed their way in
Unwanted, unwelcome
Pervasive stranger who took what was not given
Or words spoken harshly in anger
Maybe not meant but when you're young
They brand your skin so much more easily
You've not yet been tempered in life's harsh fires
Words stay, pain doesn't fade, you remember the lessons taught to you.
"You're a mistake, you're a stupid fucking cow, you're no one's first
choice."
How am I supposed to think I'm worth something
If these were the first things I learned?
The marks are inside you now
Dark stains that don't wash away
They stay
And come to mind whenever you think it's all going well
Dragging you back to the hell that is the shadows of your mind
"They won't care, you disgust them, you're so needy, they'll leave you,
no one wants your love."
You can't silence that voice
No matter how hard you try
The venomous lies it spits out
Drowning out the truth of what you know
You try hard not to let it show
How much you are hurting
How terrified you are
Of someone knowing the depth of your scars

Of that horrible voice in the back of your mind
That tells you you're worthless
You're just a nuisance
To be used and cast aside.
My scars are open
They've never fully closed
And there's not much I can change about that
Except to those who know
How bad it's been
And how hard I try
To keep that voice at bay
These are the people who want me to stay
They see the torn and bloodied parts of me
And still they love who I am
A soul in need, a heart that bleeds
And footsteps in the sand
I am who I am.

Abdul-Ahad Patel

Other Side of The Moon

Concrete floor
Brittle grains
Hold my sole until the sun sinks
Drink the lies of the clouds that
promised you fountains, but gave you
tears
The darker the night the rougher the
surface.

Darryl John

Out Of Luck

Crystal ball tell me life is beautiful,
black cats and tarot cards
explain why this life is hard,
unicorns run away,
the Blarney Stone remains cold to me,
no rabbits foot or yellow brick
road, no red shoes to take me home
the sprites in the forest leave me lost
the gods let out a belly laugh
as I try to find the path to take,
left my lucky dice behind, crawled
all over but I couldn't find a four leaf clover
ladybugs won't land on my hand,
the crickets stop chirping,
can't find a lucky penny or a wishing well,
this rope is the only thing that I have.

Chris Barber

Out of the Groove

I was lucky, this is the only negative way that the Covid-19 pandemic affected me.

Some pretend to be
experienced misanthropes,
they're fine with it all, that's
all good, it helps 'em cope,
but won't someone take me
to funky town?
There's preaching, teaching,
publicly beseeching, tribal
prejudice, knew it would
come to this, neighbours
hateful or grateful, malice
a forethought in funky town.
Started loving the quiet
restfulness, the breather
given nature and there's
talk of a shift in the culture.
Me? I'm a social animal, my
needs are fairly minimal.
I miss funky town.
Music's not the same on
your own, on silent discos
I always frown, shared
experience, nil by mouth
nutrient, yes there's some
prurience, that's funky town.
How I yearn for a great live
show, or Northern all-nighters,
though I know I must wait for
now, that don't stop me wishing
and how, that the gates are
thrown open, to funky town.
Heroic deeds by unarmed

warriors, l gratefully concede,
are now all that matters, but
I long for an end, when I can
see friends and family, celebrate
musically, turn up the volume
in funky town.
Music, company, spoken word
too, are you missing me?
I'm missing you.
Don't wanna re-program to stay
at home, or become a techno
drone. Looking forward to the
opening of funky town.

Carolyn Black

Pension Envy

Freud may have been a fraud
But his theory of penis envy
Makes sense
Now we WASPI women
View older friends
With pension envy
How come they have whoppers
And we do not?

Jason Conway

Phoenix in Flight

We huddle close to ponder
Around a roaring golden fire
To celebrate in worship
The passing of the sun
And the silence of the night

With a glass of blood red wine
And a dance of swirling flames
Under a navy star filled sky
I raise a toast to the sparks
As the Phoenix takes flight.

Scott Cowley (aka Rusty Goat)

Poetry About Tea!

It is life
It is relaxation
From the first cup
to the last sup
The last sip
Squeezing out every drip
until the pot is dry.
It is invigouration
It is concentration
They say a nation was built on it.
But the places I choose to sit with it
and I do have my favourites.
The coffee shop on the corner
McDonalds for a late night one
or an early-morning-er
The lounge at the Deveer
and the Darkroom, a place which
I will always hold dear.

It is life
It is invigouration
It is simply Tea!

Devlin Wilson

Poetry in the Park

I maintain social distancing
By reciting my own verses
Whenever I leave the house.
It's incredibly effective.
Yesterday I staged
An impromptu performance
Of poetry in the park.
Joggers, dog walkers
And casual promenaders
All fled as if pursued
By jet propelled disease pathogens.
Yet the only airborne contagion was verbal;
Flaccid rhythms, twisted syntax,
Skewed imagery and blurred meanings,
Tossed salad rather than tour de force,
Even for a self-uninvited audience.
This leads to the inescapable conclusion:
My poetry is a pestilence.

Kuma San

Rain

It's raining still and again.
Ditches full to brimming.
The quietness of once busy roads echoing on glistening surface,
Water stretches its fingers embracing fields, hedges, buildings,
clawing at carefully laid tarmac arteries.
The maw of its curiosity swallows vistas drawing clouds and sun to
earth in glowing reflection.
Dampness sharpens blustery air...
Sounds slosh, squelch...
Under umbrellas...we wait for winter to drain away.

Adele Ogiér Jones

Rebelling

And I heard the earth groaning
this is not the end remember,
though there is only so much I can do
to heal the pits they delve and carve
in my heart,
my bowels retching
rebelling
calling to the wind
to return
with new birdsong.

Jonathan R Muirhead

Recurring Dream – Draft 1

I walked again
Old streets last night
My chest puffed out
As if for a fight
I know not what
I was looking for
Be it a mild servant
Or worthy successor
I was in among streets
I did not know
That stirred in me
A melancholic glow
I was dressed as if
For a job interview
And who knows, it
May have been with you
I was coming home
For the right reasons, it seemed
The sky was blue
The sun it gleamed
And yet, I know not
Where I had arrived
My smile it fell
My heart it decried
As the streets grew and curved
When I travelled along
My home was nowhere
The buildings had gone
As had the fields
Where once I ran free
New houses and roads
Meant nothing to me
I was loyal to them

Those I'd kept in my head
The memory was true
The reality was dead
I rode on a bike
I'd had as a child
The sun kissed my cheeks
The wind it was mild
As I sailed on past family
Now long gone and dead
Having conversations still
With them in my head
For I saw them as they were
Not what they wanted to be
In that moment they became
More vivid to me
I laughed with them and joked
I hugged them and I cried
I told them what they'd got wrong
And correctly prophesied
And rode on further still
As the scenes floated and merged
My memories they faded
My visions they converged
As more developments flocked on
Invading field and playground
The kids will miss out now
But financial planning's sound
And my eyes then sadly lifted
As a new day's dawn did break
This was only a dream
But it was there for my own sake.

Adam Horovitz

Rock
For Rick Vick

I remember our first meeting
only vaguely now, more as sense-memory
stiffening to shale, becoming the past's
bedrock, essential and unmoving
under the still waters of time.

So like my father you were, and yet
not my father. It was easy to be friends.
Despite the difference in years,
we shared countless landmarks
on our tangled paths to knowledge

and age does not matter anyway.
I have watched you weather into rock,
into the Old Man of Hoy, a signal
for passing ships that they're travelling
in a good direction, yet nothing

has dimmed the blue fire of your eyes.
Memory plays tricks, brings up
the strangest moments. You pinched
my cheeks once, laughing at something
stupid that I'd said, as if I were a child.

A few weeks later, I did the same to you.
I remember the blue-skied winter
that blazed for a moment; then you laughed
like cracked ice falling into the river's rush,
the free and easy multitudes of spring.

There is so much still that could be said
over campfire coffee and honeyed toast.

So many verses and secrets, orphans
till they're shared, to be wound out
through smoke across your kitchen table.

Time is unkind, yet memories persist.
They nudge at me now like schools of fish
slipping in and out of reefs, emerge playful
as light from the cracks in the rock
that you have become. Have always been

Nick Lovell

Santa Stop Here

Santa stop here, by the car that doubles as a home.
By the blankets and boxes piled by the bins,
Where the homeless die alone,
By the shop doorway, the donated tent.
By the mate's spare bedroom or sofa.
By the council B 'n B, where they can't afford the rent.
Santa, stop here, in the squalid stinking squat.
In the derelict abandoned house
In amongst the damp, disease, and rot.
In the knocking shops and massage parlours,
barely earning enough to stay alive
In the roughest, darkest council estates
Where to survive you fight and you fight to survive.
Santa stop here, where depression is a way of life,
Where one drink is never enough, but always too many,
Where you are on the needle or the knife
Where the tree is bare of Christmas delight
Where the lights and water are both turned off,
Where it's just more of the same old shite.
Santa stop here, in the prison visiting room.
Where the hungry mouths outgrow the money
And the bills always seem to come round too soon.
In the sewers, camps and orphanages, beside the busy railway tracks.
Come on Santa, Stop here, where you are needed the most by those
who've fallen through the cracks.

Charlie Markwick

Saying Goodnight
thanks to Elizabeth Squires for introducing me to the Rondelet.

I miss Grandma
The boy said from the top bunk bed
I miss Grandma
It hurt like scratching at a scar.
I quelled the roaring in my head.
Then two wee girls chimed in, each said
I miss Grandma.

Carol Sheppard

Sea Salt & Stale Fish Guts

Sea salt and stale fish guts hang heavy in the air.
I can taste it on my lips and in my throat;
hints of mackerel, crab and lobster.
A mottled cat tiptoes along the harbour wall on silent paws.
If I hadn't caught sight of the dark shape moving in front
of the white sailing boats, I would never have known it was there.
Shop keepers bring down shutters on the day.
Families retreat from the beach, slam their doors
on buckets and spades, sandy picnic blankets,
kids crying, tired out from too much fun.
Engines start and cars roll out of town
while gulls circle above in the fading light
searching out a dropped sandwich, a cold chip.
I waited for over an hour in the creeping sea mist
But you never appeared.

Annalisa Jackson

Sesquipidalian

I've learned life is ephemeral, fleeting, fugacious
So use time to talk, be verbose and loquacious,
Just don't pontificate, prevaricate or choose to vacillate,
That's the three ways politicians communicate.
Be a logophile, learn to love language and word,
So you can share the amazing things you have heard.
When you rub your eyes those colours are phosphenes,
A word becomes interesting when you know what it means,
Some things are ineffable so no word will do,
But language isn't esoteric and only for the few,
Try psithurism, the sound of the wind in the trees,
How beautiful there's a word for a leafy breeze.
Sussuration, a whispering like rippling brooks,
And vellichor, strange wistfulness of a store for used books.
Bombination, a buzzing like a bee in flight,
And aurora, the dawn at the end of the night.
Whether komorebi, the sunlight that filters through trees,
Or chthonic the world that nobody sees,
Enjoy elysian views of bliss and delight,
And serein, the fine rain from a clear sky at night.
Whether you're a thalassophile and you love the sea
Or have eleutheromania and long to be free,
Enjoy intense happiness, joy and felicity,
From the chance occurrences of serendipity.
Coddiwomple - travel purposefully to a vague destination,
And experience metanoia, a spiritual transformation,
Don't be dogmatic, it may not be true,
Notice sonder, passers-by who have a life as vivid as you.
Life can be liminal, on the edge of all things,
Be a scintilla, a flash in the darkness it brings.
Don't be atelophobic and fear imperfection,
Be vagarious, proudly erratic in direction.
This epoch is short and soon to be gone,

Find quarancia the place where your strength is drawn.
Be mythopoeic and always make your own myth,
From the paracosm - the mind that you travel with.
Words can be spurious, terrible and cruel,
But to end on slang parlance they are all pretty cool.

Tish Camp

Share Obama's Portrait

*Outrage at the resistance of president Trump to having Obama's Portrait in the White
House, a right that was and remains denied and likely until Trump is out of office*

Trump, everything you do is shite
you're a racist, inept psycho/sociopath
on the ropes in presidential campaign
almost ready to go
down, knocked out.

You out and out weird dinosaur
with a capital 'C' (work it out)
U, that no-one wants to see
the day after Monday, next week.

Obama is the first Black President, stood tall, replete in history
unveiled in a portrait
that you now deny?

Can you feel his Black arse?
warming the seat
that he took before you?
his Black hands on the desk
did you move his furniture out?
Did you disinfect, not inspect
the Blackness of his
cocoa buttered skin
left in air behind?
Did you have others clean
his Black aroma out?

Trump, a disgrace
that can't bear to look
at that Black face
hanging in the WHITE HOUSE.

You have decidedly unveiled
yourself to be
the cowering fool in campaign
that teaches you nothing
about your mistakes
Black Vote not needed
now at all.

As proportionally the covid
beast still eats
Black Brothers and Sisters
at speed
and chokes on the
fries on the side
swallowing on poorer whites
that the herding immunity
going large McD
has cold, over ice.

I don't care that he
didn't do this or that
I care that he got there
not how he might have
fucked up, sold out
or didn't give back
he got there
in a presidential chair.

So Trump, get this
Share Obama's portrait
unveil it to all
he got the right to hang
on the fucking wall
not some tree
strange fruit Billie sang
stranger truth in your deny
because all can see
your overseer power

failing in past
cotton fields
of your final hour.

Z. D. Dicks

Skadi Hunts

This is a poem about Skadi, the Jotunn, after she realises her father was killed and makes her way for revenge.

Her hair plumed
hips snow-shod
a lithe wind whip
brushing her bow

Knives and swords
on a curved lip
her tongue crackled
a hot avalanche

she smouldered down
skiing the mountain
a clot of acrid heat
cloying molten slush

The coldest goddess
scorched in sweat
searched for prey
kindled by her wake

Matty Blades

Smallest Spark

The path is long
With twist and turns
The light it may turn dim
However grim it seems to get
A life it can be found
There's always light
In the darkest nights
Just search and you will find
The smallest sparks can set a blaze
In that darkness I have found.

Carol Sheppard

Sonnet to the Sheep of Raglan Farm Park

And when the world fell silent, deathly still,
each person told to safely stay inside,
the flock descended from the rocky hills
to Raglan Park to play on swings and slides.
They didn't worry where the children were;
jumped upon the roundabout, having fun.
The circle spun, 'til wool was just a blur,
more joined in, warmed in weakened April sun
Isolated people gazed from windows
while fleece-backed ovines grazed and dogs just barked
children cried, begged to be allowed to go,
jealous of the wayward sheep in their park
But little did they know of life just then,
the world would never be the same again.

Chloë Jacquet

Sounds of Easter

Sausages sing a song of sizzle and spit
backed by huge flames from a BBQ lit
with too much lighter fluid
A lady worries food poisoning is a risk.

The gardens are bathed in the retro electronic
pulses of the music
from the foreign family's
giant conservatory.
Upbeat and engaging
it sounds like something
made with an eighties Casio keyboard
but it is the welcome and welcoming
aural shawl
laid over the neatly boxed green spaces.

A small boy sobs for the football
that suddenly
and unexpectedly
popped when it
got kicked
into the hedge that is too spiky
to hide Easter eggs in.

Mother and aunt's hearts crack
for that inconsolable little soul
but are quietly relieved for their own.
Running around whilst drinking
gin and tonics only makes the alcohol
course through your veins faster.

The little girl calls with her eyes over the fence
wishing she could play with the boy
who doesn't speak her language.

Dandelions and daisies riot everywhere,
their colours clamouring to be seen.
Meanwhile, the forget-me-nots
mutedly remind everyone not to omit
to wake
the dormant lawnmowers.
The grass is really getting too long.

Grown-ups stay up
late into the night.
Their voices drift skywards
on the scent of smoke and weed
towards the open skylights in the roof
under which those trying to sleep kick off blankets
in the heat.

Gemma Crow

Spirit Level

Like a giant spirit level swept through the masses,
Totally ignorant to wealth or assets,
Disregarding race or religion or colour,
Indifferent to gender or age or scholar.
Flipping what we value right on its head.
This viral leveller putting malevolence to bed.
Where we once looked up to wealth and glamour,
We now stand to applaud care and honour.
The front line now the only line that counts,
The finish line, the dead line and all other lines denounced.
Humility inducing this leveller spans,
As it forces enemies to concede and join hands,
Petty disputes put into perspective,
Survival now being the only objective.
A common cause has balanced the scale,
Given us a chance to pause and exhale,
A giant audit of what we hold dear,
Of what we covet and what we fear.
I pray I take these lessons into many tomorrows,
And tread mindfully and carefully into the future I borrow.

JLM Morton

Sunday Service: Winter Swimming
Waterland Poet in Residence 2020 - January

Unscrew the lid and the steel flask rings like a singing bowl
calling the body to this winter ritual of fixing broken frequencies.
Steam from the enamel cup mists the windscreen
and we swig the coffee down, bittersweet and eager,
hot enough to relieve the brain's thinking.
Dry Robes slither off the arms, hang on lakeside pegs
and we smirk each time at the sign: No Recreational Swimming.
Toes in, soles of feet laid down on the limestone shingle,
followed fast by ankles and calves, knees and thighs and hips
and pause at the waist
to draw breath, to exclaim, to lower palms to the bream-fin grey
of the icy mirror to the luminescent reeds,
black cormorants, conifers on the near horizon.
Goggles on. Brace. Go. Push into the navy deep,
scuds of shallow waves at the neck.
Hands sweep from prayer to embrace.
Face in, eyes open to the brightening clay floor,
a copse of weed in the water's glacial clarity
glaucous and strange, a beatific underworld.
This lake has played, bred, killed, fed, held –
our ecstatic skins sing in praise and we drum the yellow buoy
in devotion to this heathen mass,
immerse ourselves in this instant, this place, this body of flesh and
water.
Turning toward the shore, we observe the coda of submerged birch
hail again the marvel of the white magpie in its branches
give thanks for this time out of mind, this chattering spirit of renewal.

Anne-Marie Kurylak

The Insane

The insane, inane, fundamentally flawed brain
Overthink and overwrought
With every overwhelming thought
Stop this madness, this broken machine
That tells me I'm replaceable
Forgettable
No one's dream
People care, they're always there
That darkness tells me I'm wrong
So I over analyse, romanticize
And internalise that thought
That idea, I'm pushed by the wayside
Lost all pride
Run and hide
Because my brain tells me I'm not required
Hard wired to think the worst
Like I'm cursed
Someone better will come along and
Like the words of some forgotten song
I'll become some abstract memory
A ghost of me
Living in purgatory
A shadow of what I used to be.
But I hold on
Try to be strong
It isn't easy to fight what's wrong
In my head
But my heart knows more
A quieter voice
That reminds me to rejoice
In my own warmth
That others see
Hold my head high with dignity

Revel in the uniqueness of me
And remember that I'm one of a kind
And though my mind may try to find
Some abstract reason to make me doubt
I say that I won't be pushed out
I'll shout from the rooftops
That I am here
I won't live in fear
And though some may say that
There are more fish in the sea
There is no one and nothing quite like me.

Jan Illingsworth

The Nest

The Orchard Hideaway:
In waist high grasses,
Under abundant trees,
Through grasshopper vaulting grounds,
Beneath summer, cerulean span,
White clouds breathe on sky-high breeze,
In cotton dress, barefooted, I ran.
The overturned rust-red water tank,
My haven from a scolding voice,
In constant unhappiness harangue.
Here in this shady hide,
Teddy and I sit side by side,
Looking out into nature forms moving.
Shushing soft sounds soothing.
A small world of secrets.
Perhaps I'll sleep here tonight,
Beneath inky skies with stars country bright?
Away from nightmares in my sleeping head.
Away from the witch under my bed.
Hugging my knees as spiders said, " No!"
If I die before I wake,
Who then unknown my soul will take?

Kelly Owen

The Power of an Honest Poet

I am tired of being polite.
I'm tired of bottling what I think.
Don't care if words press on your head.
Like a foot to help you sink.
You should not be wrapped up.
Like a delicate little flower.
I don't care if my words hit a nerve.
Honest poetry is a power.
If you don't like the way things are.
As I hit you with the truth.
I don't care if you're shaking with anger.
I don't care if you hit the roof.
Every poem that flows is honest.
I won't blow dishonest mist.
Poetry that packs a punch.
More powerful than any fist.

Josephine Lay

The Slap

Boris Johnson refusing to consider sacking Dominic Cummings for breaking lockdown regulations

He stands behind his lectern
that pillar of wood
he leans on
and delivers his blows.
Each word
slapping
bare faces
cutting ties
undermining foundations.

Betrayal
has never been so publicly
aired.
In every isolated home
the bomb blast
shudders
efforts to be brave.

Hearts beat with anger
where resignation and resilience reigned
just seconds before.

Sheena Dell

The Unclaimed Kiss

The kiss
Hung in the air;
Unpressed, unclaimed,
Integrity
Somehow maintained,
The chance let pass.
The choice
Hung in the air
And
In a thousand realities
They kissed,
But not in this, no,
Not in this.
But as their lips
Declined to touch
Each felt the gentle brush
Of breath;
And, once alone,
Each wondered if
They'd chose rightly,
Or if
They should have claimed
The kiss.

Ben Ray

The World's Oldest Periodic Table

Here's the 1st draft of my poem on the world's oldest periodic table, found under the floorboards of a house in Scotland

We never really react well together, you and I.
Acidic, you called me, tongue coarse as a scouring pad
when I chastised you for coming back too late.
Your 'little atomic bomb': we were destined to destruct.
Who knew we were living above a paper-thin slice of historical irony?
They say opposites attract – I thought our poles had aligned
that night you drew me close and our breaths mingled
as we shared our secrets, our shame.
The local historian explained why it was in German, and how
in your eloquence, it had "got tha fuck up tae Scotland."
The same way I did. Chemicals and bad luck.
All those years we had fought: a natural imbalance
playing puppet to the elements under our feet.

Nick Lovell

This is Our Today

I don't know what to say anymore.
I watch with my jaw on the floor
as people die on the streets,
Kids go to school
without enough to eat,
Pensioners can't afford to heat their homes
While leaders lie through their teeth.
Hiding the fact they've cut so deep
Cut into the bones
So they can suck the marrow.
Feathered their todays
With your tomorrow.
No sorrow or remorse for
pushing austerity onto the already poor,
while shareholders and corporations
Pay less, less, less
While taking more, more, more.
Less in wages, relying on benefits
to make up the shortfall
while their stock soars
in the financial pages.
Less in tax, expensive accountancy
bordering on criminality
allowing financial dishonesty
with limited responsibility.
Less in accountability. Legions of lawyers
deployed to defer liability. Complex contracts
referring all complaints to a third party.
Torturous trails keeping corporate crimes concealed
Company confidentiality a shield to ensure
embarrassing information is never revealed.
Truth and justice sold in hidden deals sealed
with million dollar handshakes.

They have their cake yet still eat ours.
Earning more by doing less
while we work longer hours
to keep the powers that be
away from our doors.
Kids growing up, thinking carpets are posh
and hunger is normal.
While the arms trade mongers war to fill
their coffers yet no one offers
to fill hungry children's stomachs.
How can that be right?
They are building blight through fear
of our neighbours.
Hate for our brothers and sisters.
Hardship can bond or break.
Cause friendship or abrasion
bring laughter or blisters
popping like friendships
put under the strain
of striving to survive.
We are told we have no worth,
from birth to the long house in the earth
we are valued in currency. Weighed
in workability. Sold into financial slavery.
Working for longer for a pension that's smaller
thanks to bankers still claiming their bonuses
despite destroying so many lives.
Cameras spy and pry as police
draw batons, provoking protester's voices
objecting to the choices of the chosen few
who rely on the police to do their dirty work for them.
Heads get cracked for stating the simple fact
that the system doesn't work for the many any more,
but just for the few
But any excuse will do as courts
play fast and loose with the laws,
their progress down that slippery slope
gaining applause from the right,

revelling in their might.
They are destroying our communities
restricting our opportunities to break the chains
of poverty. Blocking up the holes,
locking all the doors before
auctioning off the keys to the highest bidder
before we ever knew they were for sale.
And we rail against the system but can anything change?
Can we rearrange the order of priority in favour of humanity?
Replace trickle down economics with trickle up wealth?
Swap shareholder dividends for a real national health?
Consider our ability to share, to enjoy, to love, to smile, to dream
more important than our ability to work and barely cope?
Or is it too late, are we left bereft of all
but hope?

Viva Andrada O'Flynn

Time Will Come

time will come
when wounds numb
no longer feel pain
no longer hear pounding of rain in your heart
no longer feel betrayed
when blade dissects friendship
no longer feel need to please
and appease those who doubt you
no longer feel inferior to people supposedly superior
no longer feel hunger for fame, glory, power
it will all blur
when you're stronger
when you're braver
to be you.

Viva Andrada O'Flynn

Tonight
For World Poetry Day

Tonight, I write
of love and hate
of pleasure and pain
of sunshine and rain.

Tonight, I write
of wrong and right
of death and life
of struggle and strife.

I write worlds of words
weave my dreams
like spider's silken thread
unleash thoughts in my head

I write
Tonight.

Tish Camp

Trapped
Experience of local flooding in Tewkesbury from a 'city girl' perspective

The roads were shin deep as
floods took their toll on cars
no wellies, she took the higher paths
making her way for milk and fags.
This was no country girl
unprepared, city centric in
designs of nipping out
her roads are edged with flooded brown,
knee deep in detours of police signs.
She's rich in mud and getting back
saw how pretty the watery reflections were
as if a day tripper
she snaps away pic after pic.
A car boughs up a tidal wave
ankles wet, like a seaside day
gone wrong, the silt not sand
in her shoes, and no sun is kissing her.
Return the way she came
wetter and faster in watery dusk
reflected in headlights of speedboat cars,
hoping to get home, before they and she are trapped.

Tish Camp

Turquoise in the Haul
Grief poetry - Tears for a husband remembered

Near the top they reside
on the surface they bask
over delicate hammocks
beneath eyes, the cheek
of which, calls for their fall.
Absorbed again, a memory
tells of being alive
the we, in captured
photographic smiles
remain in horizon visualised
Welled eyes, enticed
in turquoise of Greece,
like tiny silver shoals caught
in each, the haul to fall
half-inch from the surface
or roped up in the jib
salty and anchored in you,
always.

Derek Dohren

Uncle

"Pall bearers ready"
We stand
lined up
and in unison
we lift carefully
three of us on the left.
Each of us settles the great weight
onto a shoulder.
Three of us on the right
and carefully we turn
towards the congregation.
I was seven years old
when you came to the house
on your push bike.
I expressed my fascination
and you asked me if I wanted
to go for a ride.
You lifted me over the crossbar
and climbed onto the saddle
securing me between
powerful forearms
as you reached for the handlebars.
Through the back-yard door
we went into the alleyway
and out onto cobbles
your enormous strength
and skill
keeping us upright
and all I had to do
was be
as we cut through
the silver grey of Anfield.

How odd that we journeyed
in silence.
As we make our way
out of the church
my mind hurries back
to that childhood memory.
Now I return the favour.
I carry you
as you once carried me.
I'm the strong one
keeping us upright
and all you have to do
is be
as we cut through
the silver grey of the church.
How odd that we journey
in silence

Peter Lay

Valentine's Day

As young lovers exchange cards
And exotic
Sometimes erotic
Gifts
Think of those in troubled times
With lovers
Husbands and wives
Dying
And those with cards in a memory box
Now abandoned
Left behind
Alone.

Devlin Wilson

Verboten

I am grieving for the ones I have yet to lose
In the belief I should apologise for so many things
It is decreed even the humdrum pleasures
Must be denied us now
Every touch is a transmission
Every breath an ultimatum
Each heartbeat maps the growing space between.

Henry Farrell

What's Deep Inside

It is the…
embrace in dance
That be! the rhythm of your music,
The aim of your stare,
The closeness of your steps-
With the notion in your heart...me!
And o'...talk to me baby!
I have been around,
But never known one
Who's care for me...
Speaks so loudly, as yours do:
Come! and hope be,
This dance will be our always 🖋

Belinda Rimmer

'Wrecker'

She tucks a strand of hair into her ribbed hat;
the wind has an itch, a liking for blonde.

Light from the lantern draws her face to shadow.
She's dressed in dark blue for season, quality of sky.

Fog hangs, greasy, not too solid.
She remembers a time it came down so thick

ships couldn't see her flame, bright and tempting.
Tonight, luck prevailing, a ship will sweep in,

not just up on the rocks where her light swings
but run aground, bowed as rickets,

spitting out its gold and silver and pearls,
its whiskey, rifles, tubs of tobacco.

Chained to the sea, to what it might gift her,
she never hears the curdled cries

of sailors, or thinks how scary it might be
at the bottom of an ocean.

Ann-Marie Kurylak

You Are Enough
In honour of International Women's Day

Ladies!
Do you ever feel as though
The body you have isn't quite up to the mark
That the industry says we need to achieve
In order for others to like what they perceive?
We stand at the mirror and note every flaw
That can be covered or corrected
With a jar of medical science you can buy at the store.
You must have flawless skin!
You must be tan and thin!
God forbid you should have hair anywhere except on your head
And of course, to avoid showing your age, don't go revealing any greys.
But this is all bollocks!
Who gives a fuck for perfection?
This game is insane
The only intention is
To make you feel like less than the woman you are
Take a look in your mirror and try to truly see
How unique and wonderful it is just to be
Your own glorious self
Love your thighs that always seem to kiss, your butt that will not quit cos it rocks!
Hips that curve so well
The swell of your breasts, big or small
Love them all!
Worship yourself like the goddess you are
You're warm and you're funny, you're sexy and smart
Don't chase perfection, it's a quest that is doomed
It doesn't exist
Except to persist
This perpetual myth

That unless you conform to this impossible ideal
Your identity as a woman is not real.
Be all that you dare to be!
Love every stretch mark, love every scar, love every delectable fold and
embrace who you are!
Don't be ashamed, don't hide all that wonder
Don't let the censure of haters pull you under
You are divine, say it with love
And always remember that
You are enough!

Peter Lay

42 days to Japan

42 is my favourite number, it is after all the meaning of life, and yesterday (27th March 2020) was 42 days before I was due to fly to Japan for the 4th time, hence the title…

Confined in my prison
with crap television
Beyond the window
deserted streets
a strange dystopian view
Friends, family, lovers
distant, unknown futures.

Sunshine has brightened the mood
Getting into the garden
Lifting spirits
People are scared
Where will this end?

Patched up the fence
between us and next door
their fence broken
left after the storms
our cat, Charlotte, is frightened
a gap in her domain
So, we filled it
temporarily, in the sun
a simple task completed.

Now, I sit in front of a sea of faces
a map of Japan behind me
writing words, today's words

A crow in the garden
no, there are two
black and menacing

moving in
on the resident pair
of magpies.

Clive Oseman

666 Notifications
a first draft

Hi. I'm here to deliver
your daily dose of derangement.

You see, we've come to an arrangement
but you're too slow to cotton on,
and to my amazement you treat me as important
like a long lost love you long to see-
You think of little else but me.

You think I'm there for you
to help you through the lonely times
but really, I'm there to twist your mind,
seek all the weak points I can find
and apply the pressure until they break,
gradually raise the stakes
until you can't afford to play.

I am a drug. I lure you in with short lived pleasure
and soon you will depend on me,
treasure the time we spend together
but fail to notice the subtle changes in my tone,
still see the mirage of my friendliness
but not my heart of stone.

Your world's a complicated mess,
you're searching for relief
from a relentless diet of stress and grief.
You have this naive belief in me,
but I'm a thief.

I steal your illusions one by one
and take you on a trip,

a mystery ride to my darker side
until your thoughts mirror its gloom.

You bought into it
now one assumes you knew
there was a price to pay.
You need me. You know you do.

Don't ever say we're through
because I'll make you look a fool,
like a gambler having that last bet
when deep down they know the score
that to their regret
there will always be one more

The Poets

Simon Alderwick

Simon Alderwick is a writer and musician from Surrey who has lived in the Philippines as well as Gloucestershire and London. He has travelled across the UK, Europe, Asia and Central America. His poems have been featured in 'Seiren', 'The Daily Drunk', 'Whatever Keeps The Lights On', 'Raised Brow' and the 'Squiffy Gnu' anthology.
He has a handle on Twitter **@SimonAlderwick**

Sally Aspden

Sally Aspden was born in North Wales and has lived in Gloucester for the last twenty-one years. She works part-time as a software developer for the NHS. Outside work she loves reading and enjoys walking by the Severn. She has written poetry, on and off, all her life, but more seriously in the last 16 years.

Chris Barber

Chris Barber was born in Bristol, but spent his childhood moving around the country, to which he attributes many of the influences in his poetry. A former front man in a short-lived Cheltenham Punk Band, Chris enjoys live performances and looks forward to their re-introduction. Chris resides in Newent with his wife and two grown up children, where he is taking forever to finish his first collection of short stories, partially distracted by the success recently enjoyed by his beloved Wolverhampton Wanderers.

Carolyn Black

Carolyn Black has a BA and MA in Fine Art. She is a writer, artist, film-maker and visual arts producer, often focussing on her passion for the Severn. "Severnside - an artist's view of the Severn" is her first book.

She has written many published articles, reviews and pieces for artist catalogues, art journals and publications. She shares blogposts regularly about her thinking process on her website.

Carolyn also makes poignant poetic films about the Severn. They can be seen on her YouTube Channel, Carolyn Black. Her film "When You Call I Shall Come" was recently selected for EathPhoto2020, and another film, "As Above So Below", shortlisted for the Trinity Buoy Wharf Drawing Prize.

E: **Carolyn@flowprojects.org.uk**
M: **07775938500**
W: **www.carolynblackart.com**
Youtube: **Carolyn Black**
Instagram: **severnsideartist**
Facebook: **carolynblackartworks**

Matty Blades

Matty Blades started writing poetry after tragically losing his sister, his first piece Wings of a dove was written for her funeral. Finding it therapeutic he continued on this path, becoming the **B¿@dЄ**.

Tish Camp

Tish Camp is a Gloucestershire based London poet/writer & theatre maker of Black Irish roots. She is published in Gloucestershire Poetry Societies' Anthologies (2018/19) and was a 2019 Gloucestershire Poet Laureate nominee. She was further, mentored by the current Laureate Z.D. Dicks.

She Featured at the GPS 'Raised Voices' to celebrate 'International Women's Day' at St Mary de Crypt, Gloucester, in February 2020.

In 2020 she was awarded a Paper Nation's commission to write as a marginalised writer for the South-West and further awarded a Writers' Mentoring Programme led by surrealist poet and artist, Ronnie McGrath in further collaboration with Bath Spa University 'Writing From Home' The Great Margin.

2020 -2021 holds exciting ventures including her continued personal transformations, the development of her work/ writing, current poetry commissions; performance, educational collaborations, London theatre projects and in the progression of her own forum theatre / arts development 'Rise up Theatre'.
See more at Facebook:
www.facebook.com/tishcamppoetwriter
www.facebook.com/riseuptheatreuk

Jason Conway

Jason Conway is a passionate eco-poet and professional daydreamer based in Stroud, Gloucestershire. Drawing inspiration from social issues, mental health and the transformative power of nature, his mission is to encourage people to make a positive difference in the world, for the protection of the planet and the wellbeing of its people.

He is a key member of The Gloucestershire Poetry Society, helping with its branding and marketing. Jason's debut collection 'Phoenix Rises' was published in 2018. He's performed at the 2000 Trees Festival, headlined at the Gloucestershire Poetry Festival and The Space In-Between Festival and has been published in 'The Blue Nib', 'Poetry Bus' and 'The Poetry Village' magazines.

Facebook **@jasonconwaypoetry**
Instagram **@jasonleeconway**
www.jasonconwaypoetry.co.uk

Scott Cowley (aka Rusty Goat)

Scott Cowley (aka The Rusty Goat) is a poet, spoken-word artist, multi slam winner, including an appearance at the Hammer and Tongue National Slam Finals at the Royal Albert Hall 2019.

Event host and organiser, promoter of local and nationally known performers, workshop facilitator and actively involved in all things relating to wellbeing and mental health within Swindon and beyond.

Scott has performed his work at open-mic nights across the country since February 2017 and has headlined and featured at many prestigious events, festivals, wellbeing and mental health awareness events and fundraisers.

Founder of "Rusty Goat's Poetry Corner" which is a monthly spoken-word night held in Swindon. This night was founded in 2017 with the idea of creating a welcoming and safe arena for Poets and Performers to feel able to share their work in a supportive environment, to hopefully be a useful tool to recovery and wellbeing.
Rusty Goat's Poetry Corner is well established on the spoken-word/poetry scene and attracts local and nationally known performers.

Scott describes his poetry as covering four key areas; Life, Crisis, Love and Discovery. And always; Opening doors for conversations into difficult subjects.

His first collection of spoken-word/poetry titled "Not Under My Breath" was released on Bite Poetry Press in July 2019.

[F] **Rusty Goat's Poetry Corner**
[Y] **Scott Cowley/ Rusty Goat Poetry**
[W] **www.rustygoatpoetry.com**

"Not Under My Breath" **www.bitepress.co.uk**

Gemma Crow

120 **Spirit Level**

Jewellery Maker – TV Presenter – Poet
www.gemmacrow.com

Lucia Daramus

76   Music of All Languages

Lucia Daramus is a Writer, Editor, Free-lance Journalist, and Artist, based in Gloucestershire. Recentley she completed her course in Creative Writing at Oxford University. Her MA is in Linguistings, and BA in Ancient Greek and Latin.

She read poetry in Cluj-Napoca, Bacau, Iasi, Bucuresti, Sibiu, Botosani (Romania), Chisinau (Republic of Moldavia), Gloucester, Bristol, Edinburgh, Stroud, Stourpaine, London, etc. (United Kingdom). Between 1993 and 2008 she lived in Cluj-Napoca (Romania) and she won some important prizes for poetry and Canadian International Poetry Prize "Gasparik". She also won an International Prize for Poetry, 2018, at The International Book Festival Dublin.
Her literary works were published in magazines in France, Canada, Romania, Germany, USA, England, Republic of Moldavia, etc.

She published 10 books in Romanian language and 3 books of poetry in English language, She also was exhibited as an artist:
Cluj – Napoca Romania (collective exhibition)
Gloucester – UK (collective exhibition)
Longfield – UK (Collective exhibition)
Cheltenham - UK (collective exhibition)
Stroud – UK (own exhibition) - ESCAPE FROM MADNESS, March 2018
Stroud – UK (own exhibition) – The Colours of Our Life, February, 2020

Lucia Daramus has a very open mind and in one of her essays – *'When The Colours Flow Over The Universe'* – she said: *You can lose your country, you can lose your land, you can lose all of your wealth , but you remain with something: you remain with your language to lament your sadness, your blue feelings; you remain with the colour to reflect the anxiety of your soul; you remain with the dance which can imagine your struggle. If all of these are kidnapped because of an ill-luck of an illness of mind, you remain with the memory of these types of creation which come from the subconscious.*

Sheena Dell

Z. D. Dicks

Z. D. Dicks has been accepted by 'Obsessed with Pipework', 'Sarasvati', 'Ink, Sweat and Tears', 'Three Drops from a Cauldron', 'Fresh Air Poetry', 'I am not a silent poet', 'The Hedgehog Poetry Press' plus many more, and is described as 'a gothic Seamus Heaney' by Anna Saunders (Director of The Cheltenham Poetry Festival).

His First and second collections, 'Malcontent' and 'Intimate Nature' were published by 'Black Eyes' in 2019.

Derek Dohren

Ever since he was born Derek Dohren has been getting older, and as he matures his poetry seems to get better and better. By the time he's 131 one imagines he'll be so good that you won't be able to get tickets to see him for love nor money.

He forms a poetic prong of the fabled *'Newent Massive'*, a rag tag collection of creatives that stalks the periphery of the Forest of Dean.

Derek lives a near monastic life of austerity and is pretty much devoid of social skills. That said, he's quite laid back and the only thing in life he really hates is golf ('it's the clothes, innit').

You may find a heavily disguised version of him driving buses through the forest, an activity from which he draws much of his inspiration. Thus, when he's not writing beautiful verse extolling the virtues of tea and cake, he simply falls back on recording the weird rituals of bus travel, rituals which have often invoked out of body experiences, alien abductions and the appearance of strange creatures on the surfaces of ponds.

His debut poetry collection, *'Everything Rhymes with Orange'* was published in 2019 by 'Black Eyes'.

He is also the author of *'Ghost on the Wall'*, the authorised biography of Liverpool FC manager Roy Evans, ISBN-13 978-1840188325 (2003), and the quasi-autobiographical *'The Cats of the River Darro'*, ISBN-13 978-1478315537 (2012).

Derek is a painter and was *Artist and Illustrator* magazine's *'Landscape Artist of the Year, 2009'*. His work and selected poetry, can be seen at **www.derekdohren.com** and the Facebook page *'The Art of Derek Dohren'*.

Henry Farrell

Vicky Hampton

Originally from Wales, Vicky Hampton is a Writing for Wellbeing facilitator and runs PIPs (Poets In Progress), a peer-learning poetry group in The Forest of Dean. Her poetry covers a wide range of themes, often exploring the natural world or looking at issues around family, loss and grief. Winner in various poetry competitions, including the Welsh International, Vicky has appeared several times at Cheltenham Poetry Festival, and her work has been published in 'Red Poets', 'Salopeot', 'Sarasvati', and in 'The Ways To Peace' and '#MeToo' and anthologies, and on the 'I Am Not A Silent Poet' and 'The Poetry Village' webzines.

Adam Horovitz

Adam Horovitz is a poet, editor and performer based in the Stroud valleys. He has published two full collections of poetry, 'Turning' (Headland, 2011) and 'The Soil Never Sleeps' (Palewell Press, 2018), 'Little Metropolis', a CD of poetry and music with Josef Reeve (2015), and a memoir, 'A Thousand Laurie Lees' (History Press, 2014). He has been poet in residence for Glastonbury Festival's official website, for the county of Herefordshire, for Stroud's Museum in the Park and for the Pasture-fed Livestock Association. He is one of Ledbury Poetry Festival's Versopolis poets and is the co-presenter of 'The Thunder Mutters', a poetry and music podcast. 'The Soil Never Sleeps' was released as an audiobook in 2020.

Jan Illingsworth

124   **The Nest**

Jan Illingsworth is an artist, singer, writer, poet, sculptor and gardener in New Zeeland. She enjoys tai chi and Mindfulness meditation, Vipassana. Life is too full to identify with being retired. Now she just does the things she loves.
http://www.heartinn.me/
Facebook: **Jan Illingsworth**

Annalisa Jackson

Annalisa Jackson is a writer and poet from Swindon. She has written since her teens, when she initially wrote the kind of teenage angst many start with. Luckily her writing matured from badly written sonnets about the boy on the school bus with the floppy hair (it was the nineties). Nowadays, having been married for 13 years, with 2 children she struggles to remember ever writing gushy poetry.

Annalisa's currently style is broadly eclectic, ranging from dark and disturbing to utter nonsense. Influenced by black humour developed from being an A and E nurse for 18 years, lifelong experience of being 'different' culminating with diagnosis at 40 as autistic, plus experience of mental illness with diagnoses of bipolar and PTSD, she writes poetry that makes people laugh and cry, sometimes together. She turned to spoken word in 2019 and in her first year took two semi-final places and a third place in her first three slams, plus charity features at Twigs and the Swindon Mental Health Festival, and features at Rusty Goat's Poetry Corner and Oooh Beehive in Swindon.

Wearing a trademark hat to perform to help combat anxiety she performs under the name of The Beanie Bard. Following retirement from nursing, she chose this as the name of the business she launched in 2020 to provide writing and photography services. She has also written a children's book titled: 'The Sky Painter', with more in progress as well as her first adult novel.

Future plans include growing of her new business as well as more publications as an author, and hopefully as a poet as she is currently compiling a collection for submission. Annalisa's work can be found at **www.thebeaniebard.com**

Chloë Jacquet

Chloë Jacquet is a multi-slam winning, multicultural, multifaceted spoken word artist based in Gloucestershire. She was 2017 Oxford Hammer & Tongue slam champion and reached the semi-finals of the National Slam Finals at the Royal Albert Hall in both 2018 and 2019. With a preference for straight talking and a penchant for rhymes and opinions, Chloë's poetry is both entertaining and meaningful. Her work deals with a wide variety of subjects, ranging from workplace discrimination and mental health, to the pressures placed on modern men, via her short-term relationship with a biscuit.

Chloë thinks name dropping is really uncool. She has supported artists such as Elvis McGonagall, Joelle Taylor and Hollie McNish and her work has featured several times on the BBC.

Chloë's first collection 'Take it by the Line' was published by 'Black Eyes' in September 2020

Chloë can be found on Facebook, Twitter, Youtube and Instagram using the handle **@ChloeJPoetry**

Darryl John

Darryl John is a Welsh poet from Cardiff. He has been writing poetry since his ninth birthday. He had a rough childhood he was bullied from the ages of nine until sixteen. This and his long term mental health issues are where he finds inspiration.

Darryl's poetry is very forthright and touches on tough topics, it is mostly dark in nature and focused on his daily battles with his own version of reality. He uses images that are very graphic and sometimes make uncomfortable reading. This is because he says 'the world is not all unicorns and rainbows'.

Poetry for Darryl is a kind of self-therapy where he shares his personal experiences in the hope that it may help others to face their own issues. Free verse is his preferred form but he does write forms but feels they are limiting. His inspiration comes from poets such as Edgar Allan Poe, in fact his favourite poem is Annabel Lee, he likes the simplicity and use of repetition. Some of the great confessional poets like Ann Sexton and John Berryman influence his writing.

Darryl has spent the last three years studying English literature and Creative Writing, he had two published poets as his tutors and with their help refined his writing style. He has had many poems published over these three years. He has had two books published but admits that now his poetry is much stronger than his earlier efforts. If you want to know more you will find him **@DarrylRealistic**

Darryl's poem, 'Green', is featured, as part of the, 'Of Earth and Sky', large-scale poetry installation project taking place across Gloucester. The poetry was submitted by Gloucestershire residents and can be seen on a vast scale right across the city to create a sculpture trail. People are able to discover and interact with this poetry in parks and public places from Mon 24 August – Sun 1 November 2020.
https://ofearthandsky.co.uk

Adele Ogiér Jones

102　Rebelling

Adèle M.E. Jones calls two places home: Melbourne, Australia and Freiburg in the SW corner of Germany. Her great, great grandparents were married in Gloucester before they came to Australia. This is why she originally started following Gloucester Poets.

Related to her international development work in Africa and the Asia/Pacific which involves technical and social writing, her poetry and novels are published as Adèle Ogiér Jones. Poems appear in anthologies including 'Mountain Secrets' and 'I Protest!' 'Poems of Dissent' (Ginninderra Press, 2019 & 2020) and 'The Blue Nib' (Issue 42, 2020). She has four published collections including 'Beyond the Blackbird Field' (Ginninderra Press, 2016).

Her poems often focus on environmental issues, especially the latest collection, 'Counting the Chiperoni' (Ginninderra Press, 2019) about Malawi where she worked for several years. She was shortlisted in the 2011 'UN Poems for Peace' https://www.un.org/disarmament/poetry-for-peace/ and both shortlisted and awarded in the 'My Brother Jack', Glen Eira Literary Awards, Melbourne. Adele contributes to new poetry groups and sites, making contact with emerging and continuing poets in many countries, and has regular writing contact with poets she knows personally though her work. From time to time she posts ongoing poems to her Facebook page:
https://www.facebook.com/adele.ogierjones

Kuma San

Kuma San lives a few miles outside Gloucester. She is a novice, lay Buddhist priest and currently runs popular, weekly online meditation sessions, using a collection of resonating instruments. Kuma is an instinctive composer, percussionist and musician, playing singing bowls, large gong and cymbals as well as rainmakers, sticks and mouth sounds to create a deeply moving, meditative experience.

Recently Kuma has turned her creativity towards words. Her poetry echoes her music and speaks of her joy of nature, her gentleness and compassion for all beings. She's become an active member of the local poetry scene, and took part in the GPS 'Raised Voices' celebration of 'International Women's Day' at St Mary de Crypt, Gloucester, in February 2020. The poem she read on that day, 'Forget Me Not 2', is in this anthology.

Ann-Marie Kurylak

Ann-Marie Kurylak would describe herself as a poet of the heart as her work stems from raw emotion. Originally from Gloucester in England, she now lives in Tilburg in the Netherlands with her Dutch partner and spends her free time exploring her Dutch home and trying desperately to learn the language.

Famous words to live by..."More isn't always better, sometimes it's just more."

Josephine Lay

Josephine Lay has a BA (Hons) and an MA in Studies in Creative English: she is a published author and poet; her most recent poetry collection is 'Unravelling' 2019. She is editor for 'Black Eyes', and heads the Gloucestershire Poetry Society.

Josephine is host at the monthly poetry event 'Squawkers' in Cheltenham but currently hosts 'Crafty Crows' the GPS monthly Zoom poetry event.

Josephine enjoys hosting and planning events, such as the GPS 'Raised Voices' (a celebration of International Women's Day) held in the fabulous St Mary De Crypt space, in Gloucester, in Feb 2020.

Josephine appreciates both page poetry and performance poetry and attempts to 'straddle' the divide, preferring to see all forms of poetry in terms of a poetical range or spectrum.

Josephine's poem, 'Stepping Stones', is featured, as part of the, 'Of Earth and Sky', large-scale poetry installation project taking place across Gloucester. The poetry was submitted by Gloucestershire residents and can be seen on a vast scale right across the city to create a sculpture trail. People are able to discover and interact with this poetry in parks and public places from Mon 24 August – Sun 1 November 2020.
https://ofearthandsky.co.uk

Twitter: **@JosephineRLay**
Facebook: **Josephine Lay**
https://www.blackeyespublishinguk.co.uk/josephine-lay-poet

Peter Lay

Peter Lay is a former youth worker, youth arts worker, international rock band manager and promoter. He now is now a publisher with the publishing house, 'Black Eyes' together with Josephine Lay.

He has co-written, with Zaiming Wang, a dual language (English/Chinese), cross cultural metaphorical conversation, 'Yellow Over the Mountain'.

He has visited Japan three times and during his trip last in November 2018, he experienced an emotional event when in Nagasaki and Hiroshima. Several poems about this are featured in his Poetry book, 'Still Tilting at Windmills' published in 2019.

Peter Lay ~ Performer, Promoter, Poet & Publisher
Facebook: **Peter Lay**
Blackeyespublishinguk.co.uk

Emma Lord

34   Dust to Dust

Emma Lord owns 'Sagacious Cat Creative', which combines her passions for writing, and photography. As a writer, Emma focuses on poetry, and short stories. As a photographer, she specialises in animal portraits, and creating fine art. Emma also produces freelance pieces – both written word and in photographic form – on a range of topics. Emma's poetry featured in the Swindon Wellbeing and Arts Festival 2019, and she is a regular performer at Rusty Goat's Poetry Corner in Swindon. A selection of Emma's writing can be found in the, 'Words To Live By 2020' anthology. Some of Emma's photographic work exploring mental health was selected for the Swindon Wellbeing and Arts Festival 2019. Photographs from her animal welfare collection have been exhibited in Bristol, London, and Beijing.

Emma was part of the GPS 'Raised Voices' to celebrate 'International Women's Day' at St Mary de Crypt, Gloucester, in February 2020

Based in Wiltshire, Emma splits her time between raising her young son, caring for the many rescue animals they share a home with, photographing and writing. Emma's personal projects use writing and photography to help raise awareness of various causes, all of them concerning subjects close to her heart. These include animal welfare, mental health, dementia, and parenting.

Emma's website is at www.sagaciouscatcreative.com, and she publishes to her blog at www.thephotographersway.org.
You can also find Emma's social media accounts on
Twitter **@sagacious_cat**
Instagram **@Sagacious_Cat_Creative**
Facebook **@SagaciousCatCreative**.

Freelance | Sagacious Cat Creative | Swindon
sagaciouscatcreative.com

Nick lovell

Nick Lovell is a part time commentator, full time optimist, half-arsed anarchist and occasional poet. He started writing and performing in 2013 and since then has won several slams across the country and in 2018 took part in the National Poetry Slam finals at the Albert Hall. He also co-hosts 'Oooh Beehive' in Swindon. He looks at life sideways, then writes about it!

His first collection, 'Ever Since The Accident' was published by 'Black Eyes' at the end of 2019

Drea MacMillan

Andrea Macmillan lives in the quaint town of Malmesbury in Wiltshire with her ever faithful rescue dog Jack. She has always loved writing and began her first novel at the tender age of seven after being inspired by Enid Blyton's 'The Wishing Chair'. She is a passionate reader and has an eclectic taste in books from the classics to modern African American literature. Her ideal way to spend the day is by the beach with her nose in a book. Her love of reading and writing paved the way to her career as a copywriter and she now runs her own business, Drea Macmillan Social Marketing.

Drea first began to write poetry in January 2019 as a way to help her process and heal from an abusive marriage which she escaped from in 2015. Her early writing is predominantly based on her experiences of that devastating coercive control and the PTSD it left her with. She is hoping to publish a short collection called "Domestic" based on the topic of domestic abuse in the near future. Nature and her love of travel feature strongly in her more recent work which explore the themes of lust, love and loss.

A strong and powerful performance poet, Drea has headlined at several poetry events in Cheltenham, Swindon and Gloucester. She enjoys reading her poems aloud and says "If I can help one person to get recognise that they are in an abusive relationship, and help them feel less alone, what I have been through will be worth it".

IG @drea.macillan
Facebook @dreamacmillan
www.dreamacmillan.com

Charlie Markwick

Charlie Markwick is a Gloucester based professional storyteller, poet and performer. He is a passionate advocate of the spoken word in all of its forms and believes in the power of words to transform lives. He is Poet in Residence at Gloucester Central Library. He runs poetry workshops for Age UK Gloucestershire and is currently part of an NHS Gloucestershire program that is developing story as a social prescription for the chronically lonely and the chronically socially isolated. He played a major role in the search for the Gloucestershire Poet Laureate. As part of that campaign Charlie conducted many of the street-based interviews on the Soundbites Week. In 2019 Charlie published his first pamphlet 'Orienteering', a collection of poetry that appears in his current show of the same name. His poetry has been published in the Gloucestershire Poetry Society 2019 Annual Anthology "Magic", in "Today I feel Hawaii" an anthology of poems edited by then Gloucestershire Poet Laureate Brenda Read-Brown and at Good Dadhood (https://gooddadhood.com). His poems about dementia have been included in a number of newsletters and training resources organised by the NHS 2Gether Trust.
http://charliem.poetrybooks.org/
http://www.yarnwhispering.co.uk/
https://www.facebook.com/OrienteeringTheatre/

Stephen Moore

Stephen Moore: I was born in Somerset in 1967. I grew up in the countryside and my early life, outside of our simple terraced family home was at its best when I was running free, escaping, within the open spaces nearby and getting my knees scraped and my hands dirty. Leaving all of this behind, in my working life I've strayed towards nearby counties and town life. My writing and photography reach towards themes of identity, personality and confidence. I am lost in landscapes and other places from time to time but still I seek that self-assurance, that for much of my life, has been elusive.
Visit **http://stephenmoorephotography.blogspot.com/**

JLM Morton

JLM Morton is a poet. Recent publications include pamphlets: 'Water and Stroud Poets Series 2', poems in Poetry Birmingham Literary Journal, 'Riggwelter', 'Poethead', 'Atrium' and 'The Lake'. Featured on BBC Upload, invited to read at Ledbury Poetry Festival, Juliette is Poet in Residence at a Cotswold Water Park lake and founder of Dialect, a new writer development agency for Gloucestershire. Between demands from her kids for high calorie snacks and wrenching another toy from the jaws of the dog, she writes whenever she can. Often while cooking.

An active member of the local poetry scene, she was part of the GPS 'Raised Voices' to celebrate 'International Women's Day' at St Mary de Crypt, Gloucester, in February 2020

www.jlmmorton.com
Instagram / Twitter: **@jlmmorton**

Jonathan Robert Muirhead (1978 ~ 2020)

Jonathan Muirhead has been writing since he was 13. His writing covers a variety of subjects, from news to family, love to things people say. He hopes you enjoy his work.

Sadly, less than a week after a discussion about the brief biography above, and the change of a poem title to what is now Mona Lisa, we heard news of Jonathan's passing... RIP big fella...

Viva Andrada O'Flynn

Viva Andrada O'Flynn delights in living an active lifestyle. Always on the go, she juggles tasks as a writer, artist, event specialist, host, and entrepreneur. Viva co-owns F*ART Fashion ART with her sister, Happy, in the Philippines. In the UK, happily married to her husband John, Viva creates special moments with Love Viva Cakes and Crafts.

Viva was awarded Creative Business of the Year 2019, International Women's Day Top 5 Business Women in the UK 2020, awarded by Women's Business Club. Viva was also one of the top winners of World Humanitarian Drive's COVID Times Poetry Competition representing the Philippines. You can follow Viva on
instagram: **vivavoom**
twitter: **@vivaciousviva**

Clive Oseman

Clive Oseman is a Swindon based Brummie who has been active on the spoken word scene since 2014. He is a multi-slam winner who has twice competed in the UK slam finals. These days he is better known for his humorous poetry and thrives on making audiences laugh, but he still has a serious side, as shown by the poems included in this anthology, and is comfortable performing a full set of comedy poetry, a full set of serious material, or a combination of both.

His third collection, 'It Could be Verse', was recently published by 'Black Eyes'.

Clive is also co-host and organiser (with Nick Lovell) of 'Oooh Beehive', a well-respected monthly spoken word night held at The Beehive pub in Swindon. Oooh Beehive has been a major player online during the Covid-19 crisis, with a monthly event bringing headliners of international renown, and a UK online slam championship which reaches its climax on December 6th.

Clive can be followed,
On Facebook in his own name, **Clive Oseman** or as **Clive Oseman-Spoken word**
On Twitter as **@Clive_Oseman** (though this is not often used these days)
and Instagram **@osemancliv**

Oooh Beehive also has a Facebook page…

Kelly Owen

Abdul-Ahad Patel

Abdul-Ahad Patel is a writer, actor and poet. Covering topics from race, culture and religion. He breaks stereotypes and acts as an extended voice for the oppressed and forgotten. Born and raised in Hackney, London. He is a writer of fiction but, has also featured in articles and is a screenwriter.

'My ambition as a creative is to make content that I will be remembered for; to build a legacy. After all, what we do in this life will be remembered through the ages.'

https://www.abdulahadpatel.com/

Ben Poppy

Ben Poppy,
Artist
Poet
Photographer

His first collection, 'Machine Tongue' is available from
http://www.resonancebookworks.com/

Ben Ray

128 The World's Oldest Periodic Table

2019 New Poets Prize winner and current Poet-in-Non-Residence for the 2020 Cheltenham Poetry Festival, Ben Ray is an accomplished young poet and reviewer from the Welsh borders with 'a fresh and original poetic voice – full of wit, twists, surprises, echoes and challenges' (Alan Rusbridger, former editor of The Guardian). His third collection, 'The Kindness of the Eel' was published with The Poetry Business this June, and has two previous collections with Indigo Dreams Publishing.

Ben's poetry, reviews and articles have appeared in a wide array of journals, newspapers and websites. From performing at sold-out venues to one-to-one mentoring and from leading poetry groups to giving talks and workshops with young people in schools, Ben is a versatile and consummate poet, performer, workshop leader and mentor.

Ben is extremely active in the poetry community, whether it's running virtual online workshops during the Coronavirus crisis, judging the 2020 Cheltenham Poetry Festival single poem competition or presenting an academic paper on poetry and climate change at the 2019 World Youth Forum: Rights to Dialogue in Italy. He has also had work commissioned by the EU Commission and performed within the EU institutions, and his workshops and poetry have also been included in the Living Levels Landscape Partnership with the RSPB.
Web address: **www.benray.co.uk**
Twitter: **@BenRayThePoet**
Email address: **ben_ray@live.co.uk**
home - Ben Ray, poet
benray.co.uk

Brian Reid

Brian Reid **@Mojoetry** is a Chippenham based DJ, MC writer and occasional actor but Spoken Word is finally his 1st love after a lifetime of denial.

Belinda Rimmer

Belinda Rimmer has worked as a psychiatric nurse, lecturer and creative arts practitioner. Her poems have been widely published in magazines, on-line journals and anthologies, including: 'Under the Radar', 'Ambit', 'Prole', 'Brittle Star', 'Dream Catcher', 'Eye Flash', and 'Ink, Sweat & Tears'.

In 2017, she won the Poetry in Motion Competition to turn her poem into an award-winning film, since shown Internationally. In 2018, she came second in the Ambit Poetry Competition. She was also joint runner-up in the 2019 Stanza Poetry Competition. She is one of the two winners of the Indigo-First Pamphlet Competition, 2018, with her pamphlet, 'Touching Sharks in Monaco' (published Spring 2019).

Belinda was the judge of the GPS 2020 Open Poetry Competition.

Twitter: **@belrimmer**

Morgan 'I'm-not-a Poet' Rye

Pinterest: **Morgan Rye** (then click on **SBEQuinn/1** etc.)

Dave Seed

David Seed is a Gloucester based artist and writer. Poetry has been a relatively recent departure for him, being an experiment in broadening his palette, and he's still learning how to mix his words to achieve the tones that he wants.

See more of his work in the Facebook page: **David Seed Scribblings** or here: **www.davidseedfineart.co.uk**

Carol Sheppard

Carol Sheppard had a children's play produced in 2005. Came second in the International Screenwriters short film script competition in 2008. Had monologue performed in Hawaii in 2009. Had short play performed script in hand with Wild Orchid Theatre in December 2009. Had poems and articles published or exhibited. Writes a weekly column for The Citizen newspaper (readership 17,000). Full length play, "The Drop of a Pin" produced in July 2015 as part of Only in Gloucester Festival by Brick Door Theatre Company and touring Gloucestershire in summer of 2016 and then on to New Zealand for a summer tour 2017. New play placed with Small Spaces theatre group and will be touring in 2021. Another placed with Our Stars Theatre Company now delayed until 2021. Had a radio play, "Jesus in the Fridge" recorded by Little Wonders Radio Plays. My short film script "Enough to make you cry" filmed in 2018.

An active member of the local poetry scene, Carol was part of the GPS 'Raised Voices' to celebrate 'International Women's Day' at St Mary de Crypt, Gloucester, in February 2020

Carol's poem, 'Journey', is featured, as part of the, 'Of Earth and Sky', large-scale poetry installation project taking place across Gloucester. The poetry was submitted by Gloucestershire residents and can be seen on a vast scale right across the city to create a sculpture trail. People are able to discover and interact with this poetry in parks and public places from Mon 24 August – Sun 1 November 2020.
https://ofearthandsky.co.uk

Alby Stockley

51   **Home Ruin**

Alby Stockley is a Poet, Spoken Word Performer and Textile Artist based in Kent. She is a regular performer at Spoken Word London with her son Elric who both Featured in their Anti Hate Festival earlier this year. Alby can also be found taking part in local Spoken Word nights in and around Kent. She recently supported at the Maidstone Fringe Festival, being introduced as an Empathetic Poet. Her topics range from LBGTQIA Advocacy, Grief and life experience with many of her writing being autobiographical.

Alby has featured at 'Squawkers' in May 2019, in the Squawkers Tag Poetry Slam in November 2019, at 'Rusty Goats Poetry Corner', Swindon in February 2020.

She Featured at the GPS 'Raised Voices' to celebrate 'International Women's Day' at St Mary de Crypt, Gloucester, in February 2020.

Marilyn Timms

13   **A Day Like Any Other**

Marilyn Timms has been widely published online and in print. Her second poetry collection, 'Deciphering the Maze', written in collaboration with husband Howard, was published by Indigo Dreams earlier this year. The book explores falling in love, marriage and loss. It charts how they navigated a way through their own and each other's cancers to a joyous reaffirmation of life.

Trevor Valentine

Trevor Valentine: Singer-songwriter, lately trying my hand at just poetry. Following the traumatic death of a friend, who I was unable to save, I didn't realise how it had affected me. But the poetry inside me did. It helped bring balance, an outlet. I have also witnessed the savagery of abusers, of all kinds. And lately, the pandemic. My poetry can often be uncomfortable. But as far as I remember, each poem has an intended message. The point of poetry, for me at least. My style is almost without rhyme, which I see as an unnecessary constraint, often getting in the way of the message. I hope to publish my first collection of poems, already having the title 'Life Sentences'. Any guidance sincerely appreciated.

Devlin Wilson

Devlin Wilson lives and works in Gloucester. He has been a member of GPS for three years.

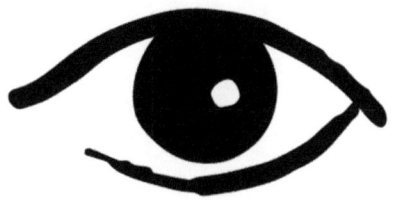

Black Eyes Publishing UK

'Black Eyes' is an independent publisher, based in sight of the cheese-rolling hill in Brockworth, Gloucestershire.

So… 'Publishing from the Edge'

We were established in 2018. Our aims are to produce a small number of exciting, and at times, alternative literature in various genres.

So… 'Quality not Quantity'

Blackeyespublishinguk.co.uk

Lightning Source UK Ltd.
Milton Keynes UK
UKHW022142021020
370930UK00005B/275